Teaching Kids to Spell

Teaching Kids to Spell

J. Richard Gentry
Jean Wallace Gillet

HEINEMANN
Portsmouth, NH

HEINEMANN EDUCATIONAL BOOKS, INC.
361 Hanover Street   Portsmouth, NH 03801
Offices and agents throughout the world

Every effort has been made to contact the copyright holders for permission to reprint borrowed material where necessary. We regret any oversights that may have occurred and would be happy to rectify them in future printings of this work.

Table 4–1	Adapted from "You Can Analyze Developmental Spelling" by Richard Gentry. In *Teaching/K-8,* May 1985. Reprinted by permission of the publisher.
Table 7–1	Table from *Teaching Reading Vocabulary, Second Edition* by Dale D. Johnson and P. David Pearson, copyright © 1984 by Holt, Rinehart and Winston Inc., reproduced by permission of the publisher.
Appendix A	*Language Arts: Learning Processes and Teaching Practices, Second Edition* by Charles Temple and Jean Wallace Gillet. Copyright © 1989. Published by HarperCollins Publishers. Reprinted by permission.
Appendix B	From Sharon J. Crawley and King Merritt, *Remediating Reading Difficulties*. Copyright © 1991 William C. Brown Publishers, Dubuque, Iowa. All rights reserved. Reprinted by permission.
Appendix C & D	Smith, C.B. and G. M. Ingersoll (1984). *Written Vocabulary of Elementary School Pupils: Ages 6–14,* pages 33–42. Bloomington, IN: Indiana University Monographs in Language and Reading Studies, no. 6. Jan.

Library of Congress Cataloging-in-Publication Data
Gentry, J. Richard.
   Teaching kids to spell / J. Richard Gentry, Jean Wallace Gillet.
      p.   cm.
   Includes bibliographical references.
   ISBN 0-435-08760-6 (alk. paper)
   1. English language—Orthography and spelling—Study and teaching—United States.   I. Gillet, Jean Wallace.   II. Title.
LB1574.G42   1993
372.6'32—dc20   92–24371
                                                                         CIP

Designed by Jenny Jensen Greenleaf.
Printed in the United States of America on acid free paper
93 94 95 96 97   7 6 5 4 3 2 1

Contents

Preface

One of the questions teachers ask most often is, "What's the most effective way to help kids become better spellers?" Parents, too, are concerned about spelling: they worry when they see their children turn in homework or compositions with misspelled words; they worry when their children get poor grades in spelling.

But spelling is not just a problem for young learners. Many adults struggle with spelling, too. Almost everyone will confess to a few "demon words" that he or she just can't seem to get right. For many adults, poor spelling means more than just encountering the occasional hard word; it can be a feeling of dread they experience every time they pick up a pencil or sit down at the keyboard. Poor spelling erodes self-confidence and can cause us to avoid writing anything, even such simple things as a thank-you note, an absence excuse, or a congenial note to a friend.

Poor spelling is not always caused by a lack of education; many highly educated, highly literate professionals such as authors, physicians, judges, college professors, and engineers are poor spellers. Poor spellers are not less intelligent, less educated, or less motivated than better spellers. But they, with countless schoolchildren, suffer through the misery and humiliation that poor spellers must face.

What can we do about it? We can start by understanding that spelling is a process. We can learn why some children seem to be good spellers naturally, while others seem stymied by spelling. We can study how children learn to spell—what they learn earlier and what they learn later in the process—and apply that knowledge to spelling instruction. We can ask what instructional strategies seem to help children as they progress as spellers, and what appears to waste their time or even make the journey harder. Is spelling largely a matter of memorization, or is it really much more complex? Can children learn to spell naturally and easily without spelling instruction, simply by extensive reading and writing? Do some children learn to spell automatically, while others need systematic instruction? What is the best way to teach spelling?

The answers to these and other questions about spelling are found here. This book will help you understand the spelling process. Whether you are an experienced teacher, a teacher preparing to enter the field for the first time, or a parent, and whether you are a naturally good speller or a poor speller, you will be surprised at the intricacies of how spelling works.

Everyone who reads or writes is a speller. Yet few of us, including teachers, understand this intriguing process. By writing this book we hope to mark a path you can follow that will help you understand, teach, and use spelling more successfully. We can't promise you'll become an expert speller, but we do promise to show you a series of snapshots of the spelling process, so that from this time forward you can say, "Now I see how spelling works!"

Acknowledgments

This book actually began about twenty years ago when the authors met as graduate students in a very special doctoral program at the University of Virginia. We acknowledge our good fortune to have studied with the late Professor Edmund H. Henderson whose work along with that of his students has helped pave the way for a better understanding of spelling. We are proud to be associated with the University of Virginia group of spelling and word knowledge teachers and researchers. Many of our readers who share a common interest in spelling will recognize these names: Carol Beers, Jim Beers, M. Jane Cooke, Tom Estes, Charlene Gill, Tom Gill, George Graham, Edmund H. Henderson, Darrell Morris, Elizabeth Sulzby, Bill Teale, Charles Temple, Shane Templeton, Jerry Zutell, and others who have followed.

A special thank you to M. Jane Cooke, Ronald L. Cramer, Carolyn Miegs, William Paulk, and Charles Temple who read parts of our original manuscript and offered helpful suggestions. Philippa Stratton provided outstanding editorial assistance, Steve Acklin was a computer genius, and Joanne Tranchemontagne provided expert production expertise. We would have been lost without Shirley Bateman and Mary Jane Farnell who typed over holidays and enabled us to meet deadlines. We very much appreciate their help.

We wish to thank our families and friends who encouraged us throughout this project and kept us smiling. Finally, thank you to Carol Fiske, Stacy Gentry, Jenny and Leslie Gillet, Dan Miegs, and many other spellers who shared wonderful samples of invented spelling.

Reconceptualizing Spelling Instruction

AT THE 1991 Whole Language Umbrella Conference in Phoenix, Arizona, Ethel Buchanan, in her presentation on spelling, expressed concern. "If anything will defeat whole language," she said, "it is what we do with spelling." According to conference participant Marytherese Croarkin, Buchanan's words "mirror the attitudes of many of the teachers I spoke with during the conference. Many of these teachers felt that the whole language model, in and of itself, does not have the structure they need to teach spelling comprehensively. They are also concerned with the public's perception of the ways in which spelling is treated in the whole language classroom—that is, that parents believe that spelling is not being taught. The teachers realize that students need to learn conventional spelling, but they fear that overemphasizing this skill goes against the grain of whole language.

"Many of the teachers who embraced other aspects of whole language philosophy," she continued, "expressed concern about the ways in which spelling is or isn't being handled in the whole language classroom. I spoke at length with several junior high school language arts teachers from California who were very disturbed by the fact that their students, products of whole language classrooms, could not spell simple words."

Whole language teachers are not the only ones experiencing difficulty with the teaching of spelling. In many traditional and eclectic classrooms teachers are dissatisfied with spelling instruction. They too express fears, concerns, and doubts about spelling and have questions that need to be answered.

At present, two philosophies of spelling education are pulling in opposite directions like the entangled lines of two kites in flight. Whole language and traditional views of spelling education have crisscrossed in an inextricable tangle of theories, attitudes, and myths. The resulting tension threatens to break both lines. We hope that *Teaching Kids to Spell,* by giving teachers an understanding of the spelling process, will help to unravel the knot. We will not hold one model and toss the other aside. Rather, we believe that ideas from both models must be used to launch a balanced consideration of how to teach spelling. Our purpose is to help you achieve more success—a smoother flight—as you teach spelling and relate it to writing and reading. Our approach will be to provide you with the information you need to set your own course. *Teaching Kids to Spell* presents information and ideas that should help you increase your knowledge, add to your store of teaching resources, and ultimately enable you to reconfirm or reposition your attitudes about how to teach spelling. It should be helpful for whole language and traditional teachers alike.

As a teacher, you have choices, and we believe you should be empowered to make them. But the time to act is now. The lines are caught, the tension is great, and both lines are in danger of breaking. Whether you double one line to strengthen it, tie the lines together in an attempt to fly higher, or separate the lines and continue to fly your own way, we hope *Teaching Kids to Spell* will help you.

How to Get Started

In order to reconceptualize spelling, we must begin with the recognition that learning to spell is a complex process. When teachers try to make teaching and learning spelling unrealistically simple, spelling instruction can be disastrous. For example, the notion that spelling is simple memorization has resulted in many failures in the classroom. Merely assigning words to be studied and memorized has been unsuccessful. Equally unsuccessful is the idea that children learn to spell by some sort of mental osmosis—that wide-ranging reading and writing will miraculously result in highly accurate spelling. Another simplistic and harmful notion is that spelling is not really important and that teachers do not need to worry about it. Not understanding spelling as a process has caused us to treat it unrealistically, and our resulting classroom practices have debilitated children. We believe the root of the problem has been a lack of understanding.

Let us begin with the recognition that learning to spell is a complex process. To explain this process, this book offers a philosophy of language learning for spelling that provides a bridge between cognitive and operant views of learning. We draw on the best information available from both whole language and research-based traditional views about how to teach spelling. The secret to a successful program is a good balance.

While some believe whole language and direct instruction models are mutually exclusive, we believe they are different but complementary. Learning to spell entails both unconscious and effortless learning as well as learning that may need to be more directed and specific. Learning to spell is an individual process. Children do not learn to spell with equal ease or in the same way. While learning the language system for spelling may be easy and natural for some children, others—including many adults—may find it extremely difficult.

An Overview

Teaching Kids to Spell provides a reconceptualization and a synthesis of both the whole language model and a refined traditional model of spelling instruction. Our goal is to provide you with information you can use to implement a spelling program that works for your classroom and for your students. We believe there is more than one way to teach spelling, and you must decide what works best for you. However, your program will be more successful if you understand spelling and follow some basic guidelines no matter what plan you implement. Twelve key elements will lead you toward a balanced, research-based theory of spelling and to more successful spelling instruction in your classroom:

1. *Treat spelling as a complex process.* Remember that part of the problem with the teaching and learning of spelling has been that we have treated it too simplistically: as a memorization task, as a list to be assigned, as learning that occurs incidentally, or as not important at all. Learning to spell is an important aspect of language,

and learning to spell is complex. Your instructional approaches should reflect these facts.

2. *Help kids meet all four demands of expert spelling.* Spelling is a complex language system with phonetic, semantic, historical, and visual demands. In the pages that follow you will learn some of the strategies for helping your students meet each of these demands.

3. *Treat spelling as a developmental process.* Early spelling skills unfold in development stages much like learning to speak, from general to specific. You must use invented spelling to set the foundation for spelling competence.

4. *Individualize spelling.* Independent, competent spellers realize their greatest potential growth when instruction is child centered.

5. *Integrate spelling in all subject areas.* But recognize that the concept of integration does not preclude the possibility of having children spend time specifically on spelling.

6. *Take advantage of invented spelling as an opportunity for learning.* Invented spelling is a powerful tool for both learning and assessment. In this book you will gain a better understanding of invented spelling, learn how to encourage it in your students, and discover new ways to use it to assess and nurture spelling competence.

7. *Think of whole language and spelling instruction as being compatible.* Many principles of whole language are used in this book. There can be a happy marriage between whole language and spelling instruction.

8. *Use instructional resources for teaching spelling.* Resources are tools for teaching. This book gives you many spelling resources—ideas and activities for the classroom.

9. *Educate parents and solicit their help.* Parents' obsession with spelling can be the bane of a teacher's existence. This book will help you lead parents to a better understanding of your spelling program.

10. *Pay attention to commonly used words.* Individuals learn to spell words. It is appropriate to focus attention on commonly used words and have children work with them in order to learn to spell them. Word study can be playful and fun. Sooner or later all children choose to write *they, too, there,* and *of;* it is appropriate for the teacher to help children identify words like these for spelling study.

11. *Remember that spellers must also be readers and writers.* Suggestions in this book are made with the understanding that children must read and write daily in a language-rich environment to develop properly as spellers.

12. *Teach proofreading and spelling consciousness.* Students must learn to proofread and edit. They must develop a desire and a concern for spelling accuracy and a habit of care for correct spelling.

Learning to spell begins with early pencil-and-paper activity. Chapter 2 focuses on the beginnings of spelling by examining the basic principles of language learning that set the foundations for later spelling competence.

Chapter 3 identifies five stages of invented spelling; chapter 4 shows you how to use this knowledge to assess early developmental growth. Sprinkled with delightful examples of children's writing and invented spelling, these chapters also treat invented spelling technically and as a science. A thorough understanding of invented spelling reaps rich rewards for practical use. The developmental spelling test in chapter 4 can be used for accurate individual analysis and assessment, and can be administered to either individuals or groups in just a few minutes.

Chapter 5 takes spelling beyond the early developmental stages of invented spelling and examines the phonetic, semantic, historical, and visual demands of expert spelling. It also provides a historical perspective of English spelling development. Since developing visual awareness is a benchmark of expert spelling, visual demands are emphasized.

Chapter 6 reviews the spelling-writing connection and outlines procedures for implementing a spelling workshop, an effective way to teach spelling in the classroom. This chapter provides a plethora of individual activities that prepare kids to meet the phonetic, semantic, historical, and visual demands of spelling.

Chapter 7 puts the spelling basal in proper perspective and focuses on how to choose spelling words. You will learn how to use basal lists and how to develop your own spelling list. This chapter also provides important tips for teaching patterns, prefixes, roots, and word etymologies.

Finally, chapter 8 provides guidelines for an effective schoolwide spelling program.

The reconceptualization of spelling is a valuable undertaking. We believe *Teaching Kids to Spell* will help you better understand spelling and how to teach it. Our aim is to foster healthy practices in the classroom and so help children become better spellers.

2

How Spelling Begins

LESLIE HAS NEVER known a time when print was not part of her life. She has been read to since she was a baby, and now as a kindergartner she has heard over a thousand different stories. In addition, she has engaged in many readings of the same stories over and over. Her room is cluttered with library books, books of her own, pictures she has drawn, signs she has made, and her own writing. One shelf of her bookcase is filled with boxes of crayons and felt pens, a can of pencils and pens, boxes of chalk and a chalkboard, and papers of all sizes. Nearly every day she sees her parents read the newspaper, magazines, novels, and mail; in addition, in the last several years she has watched as her older sister has learned to read and write. And bedtime isn't a proper bedtime without at least one quick story.

In spite of the fact that her mother is a teacher, Leslie has never been taught to spell or write. The examples set by her parents, preschool teacher, big sister, and grandparents and the print-rich environment in which she lives were enough to set her feet firmly on the road to literacy long before she entered school this year. Although she is not really reading much yet, it won't be long before Leslie begins to read naturally. But she is a prolific and enthusiastic writer. Like many children, Leslie is learning to write and spell before she learns to read. She is doing this by a natural process of figuring out how print works, by example, and by experimentation.

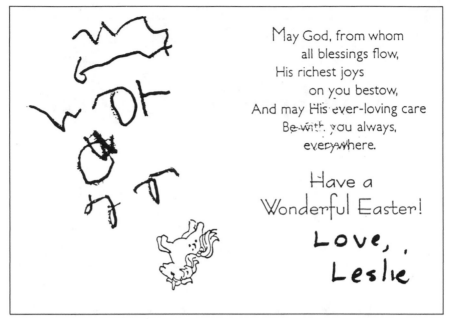

May God, from whom
all blessings flow,
His richest joys
on you bestow,
And may His ever-loving care
Be with you always,
everywhere.

Have a
Wonderful Easter!

Love,
Leslie

FIG. 2–1   *Scribbled Message and Letterlike Forms (Leslie, age 2 years, 6 months)*

The samples of spelling and writing that follow, produced by Leslie between the ages of two and six, show her growing mastery of print.

A Writer Discovers How to Spell

At 2 years, 6 months, Leslie scribbles a message on an Easter card (Figure 2–1). At this age, Leslie cannot write the letters of the alphabet, but her letterlike forms show what she already knows about aspects of print. Her scribbled "letters" have linearity, loops, crosses, circles, and other configurations of English print.

At 3 years, 3 months, while attempting to spell her name, Leslie successfully orchestrates upper- and lowercase *l*'s and an *e* (Figure 2–2). The alphabetic principle is not yet intact; Leslie's letters do not yet represent sounds. But she is expanding her letter-writing repertoire and produces a random string of *l*'s, *e*'s, *m*'s, *i*'s, *n*'s, *d*'s, and an *r* to describe her drawing of a flock of butterflies (Figure 2–3).

FIG. 2-2   *Leslie's Name (3 years, 3 months)*

A year later, at 4 years, 3 months, Leslie understands the alphabetic principle that letters represent sounds in words. She can segment words into component phonemes and can almost successfully spell her name (Figure 2–4). The alphabetic principle is clearly in evidence as she invents a spelling for *rain:* she segments *rain* into three phonemes and writes R for /r/, A for /a/, and N for /n/.

By the age of 5 years, 11 months, Leslie can invent spelling for many of the surface sounds of speech (Figure 2–5):

Message:		No	boys	allowed	
Sound:		/n/ /o/	/b/ /oi/ /z/	/a/ /l/ /o/ /d/	
Leslie's spelling:		N O	B A Z	A L D	

Message:	in	this	girls'	club
Sound:	/i/ /n/	/th/ /i/ /s/	/g/ /i/ /r/ /l/ /s/	/c/ /l/ /u/ /b/
Leslie's spelling:	A N	TH EI S	G I Z	C L U B

9

FIG. 2–3   *Leslie's Description of a Flock of Butterflies*

FIG. 2–4   *Spelling of Leslie's Name in Capital Letters and Story of a Rainstorm (4 years, 3 months)*

FIG. 2–5 *Sign: "No Boys Allowed in This Girls' Club" (5 years, 11 months)*

At this age Leslie can write much of what she wants to express; she is a semiphonetic and phonetic speller. She can also read some words. In the commonly used word *this* we see evidence that she is noticing the visual conventions of print. Perhaps she noticed *t-h* in *the* and *i* in *is, t-h-e* in *the, i-e* in *Leslie,* and perhaps *e-i* in other spellings. So why not THEIS for *this?* With the exception of her name, this is one of her earliest spellings using a visually inspired vowel digraph.

During this phase, though, many of Leslie's invented spellings are semiphonetic—abbreviated spellings representing only part of the surface sound of her speech. For example, *allowed* is spelled ALD; and, in a picture of Humpty Dumpty (Figure 2–6), *Humpty Dumpty* is spelled HMT DPD.

It is fascinating to observe Leslie hypothesize sound and word segmentation. In Figure 2–7 she comes up with a creative use of hyphens for what must have been a challenge for her: "How do I write 'huggable cat'?" We can imagine what she might have been thinking as she came up with a creative solution employing hyphens: "I'll use one of these - things!" Indeed, her use of hyphens to segment words is an appropriate use of the hyphen:

HEG–EBL–CAT
huggable cat

As a six-year-old speller Leslie demonstrates remarkable accuracy in rendering phonetic spellings of the surface sounds of speech. Her use of abbreviated semiphonetic spellings (fewer letters than sounds)

FIG. 2–6   *Leslie's "Humpty Dumpty" Picture (6 years)*

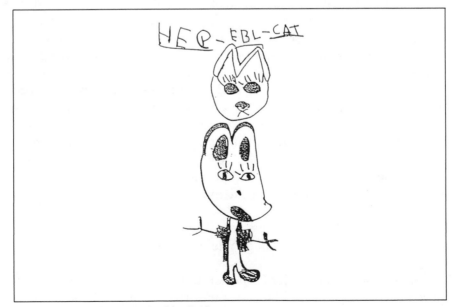

FIG. 2–7   *Leslie's "Huggable Cat"*

FIG. 2–8 *"Donald and Daisy" (6 years, 3 months). Translation: "This is a picture for Mom. I hope you like this picture of Donald Duck and Daisy Duck."*

is now rare; she now uses more complete phonetic spellings. Leslie is continuing her quest: she is learning to spell by example and by experimentation. She is more expansive, occasionally rendering a full page of cohesive text such as her description to accompany her drawing of Donald and Daisy Duck (Figure 2–8). Note Leslie's use of hyphens to designate spaces between words. For Leslie, conceptualizing what a word is and how to designate a word in print are wonderful challenges. In her writing, Leslie experiments with conventions; she decides to render "hope you" and "Daisy Duck" without space markers (HEPUOU; DASYDEC). At six, Leslie is decisively a phonetic speller: thirteen of the eighteen invented spellings in the Donald-Daisy piece are phonetic (one is semiphonetic, one is transitional, and three are correct spellings). Leslie demonstrates remarkable orthographic acumen as she slowly but surely unlocks the doors to the mysteries of English alphabetic writing. Leslie, the writer, is indeed learning how to spell.

Learning to Talk and Learning to Spell Are Related

Children like Leslie seem to learn the foundations for spelling in much the same ways as they learn to talk and use language. This is no coincidence; speech and writing are both language functions. Both are built on *imitation, invention, interaction,* and *risk taking*.

Since talking precedes writing, let's consider first how a young child learns to talk, How is it that a child moves from being a preverbal baby to a babbling baby, and then to a talking toddler or preschooler?

To begin with, it's important to keep in mind that human beings are biologically predisposed to speak; one of the things that distinguishes humans from other animals is our complex oral language systems. Although other animals communicate in sophisticated ways, many of them using sounds, no other animal species has developed as complex and infinitely variable an oral communication system as humankind has. We are built to talk, both physically and cognitively. Humans may even be predisposed to learn systems of written language—not necessarily the intricacies of expert spelling, but at least the foundations and how the system works. Let's look at some of the behaviors that lead to the construction of human language systems.

Certainly *imitation* plays an important role. Without it, we could not account for the fact that young children learn to speak the language or the dialect with the accent of the home. An infant born in Korea, for example, and adopted at birth by a couple in Birmingham, Alabama, begins to speak not Korean, as she would if she were raised in her country of birth, but English; and not just any English, but the Southern-accented English of her adoptive parents. Anyone who has spent much time with infants before they learn to talk knows that babies imitate the sounds and intonation of the language around them. Also, imitating how Mom, Dad, Grandma, and the babysitter say certain things is common to almost all children.

But infants' imitation of the language they hear is not simple or mindless; rather, it is complex. Speech is not simply imitated; it is conceptualized and reconstructed. Imitated speech is the kind of imitation that would result not in an exact parroting of what is heard, but rather in a reconstruction. The imitation uses the same elements as the speech being modeled—phonological elements (sounds), syntactic elements (nouns, verbs, and modifiers), and semantic elements (vocabulary, meaning, and concepts). These elements are reconstructed by the developing speaker through a complex developmental process. Indeed, the child is built to talk and does imitate the talk that he or she hears. But the process is not simply imitation. The new speech that results is "rebuilt speech" for which the speaker has used the same elements as the speech being imitated.

This rebuilding, or invention, of the language being imitated explains how children can produce phrases and sentences that they have never heard before. Certainly a good part of language learning involves the child's *inventing* words, phrases, and sentences that he or she has never heard, perhaps utterances that no one else has ever said. Every parent has a store of phrases peculiar to his or her own child. You yourself produced some unique language when you were a toddler. One four-year-old child, for example, had never seen a motorcycle but was familiar with bicycles and with what bikes looked like. She was likewise very familiar with the appearance and sound of her father's chainsaw, which he used for cutting firewood. The first time she saw a family friend ride up to the house on a motorcycle, she called it a "chainsaw bike," relating its noisy motor to the saw and its general configuration and function to the bike. Another child, a two-year-old, used the unique expression "smellslike" as a noun, as in her frequent question "What is dat smellslike, Mom?" Apparently she abstracted this new word from sentences she heard from her parents, such as "It smells like smoke in here" or "Smells like Grandma's baking again." This quality of invention may account for the common mistakes that young children make when overgeneralizing rules, using irregular plurals and verb tense endings they never hear from adults, such as "Look at the sheeps," "I hurted myself," or "He eated all my cake."

So we have, in children, a biological predisposition to learn and use systems of language. We also have the complex interaction of imitation and invention. But without a *language environment,* language learning will not take place. Without language in the environment, children do not become language users. In order to learn to talk, children must hear language and *interact* with others using their language. *Imitating, inventing,* and *interacting* with language are all essential to normal language development.

Interaction is important because it relates directly to later learning to write and spell. Just as children interact with oral language in order to speak, they must interact with written language in order to learn to write and spell. They must be read to and have books to look at and pretend to read. They must have their attention drawn to print in books, in advertisements, on grocery labels, and on signs. They must see adults writing things like grocery lists, birthday cards, phone messages, notes, and letters. They must have materials and opportunities to try to write, and have their efforts remarked on and appreciated. This kind of interaction with print is critical to learning to produce written language. Fortunately, it is not difficult to provide. Many parents provide this help without even knowing how important and useful it is. But for children, regardless of home experience, the classroom must provide the perfect opportunities for such interaction to take place.

An Early Spelling Lesson at School

The door to Ms. O'Connell's kindergarten classroom is propped open and the sound of creative endeavor can be heard. Young voices, movement, and snatches of laughter invite us to look in as we pass by. It is midmorning, and the children are writing. Most are working at large tables; a few lie on the floor. A few work alone, but most are working with one or two friends. Each child has a large sheet of writing paper and containers of crayons; colored felt pens and fat primary pencils are close at hand. In the center of the tables sits a large wire cage containing a gold and white guinea pig. The guinea pig belongs to Roxane, whose mother has visited the class this morning to talk about guinea pigs and their proper care. Several illustrated books about guinea pigs from the school library are displayed on the table near the cage. The last thing one might guess about all this activity is that the children are engaged in learning to spell.

As we move closer, we see that most of the children are actively writing and drawing. Most of them are talking either to themselves or to friends as they work. A few silently study the work they have done so far. A few are reading their work aloud to themselves; two are looking at pictures of guinea pigs in the books.

Steven has just finished drawing a guinea pig on his paper; taking up a blue crayon, he carefully adds a blue mask with eye holes to his

drawing, and then laughs to himself as he writes below it "MUT PIG."
Then he pokes his neighbor, chuckles, and says, "Look, it's a mutant
Ninja pig!" Darleen draws a large oval with a smiling face at one end
and two three-toed "bird feet" at the bottom. Then she selects a
purple marker and scribbles loops below the picture, murmuring to
herself as she does so, "His name is Sunflower." Roxane has finished
her picture and carefully writes below it "SEFLRESMIGENEPG." When
she finishes the final letter she runs her finger slowly under the line of
print as she reads, "Sunflower is my guinea pig." Chris breathes hard
and hunches over his paper, his pencil clutched hard in his fist as he
writes "FNHVNENFLNL" across his paper. Lolly has drawn a large
yellow and white striped guinea pig surrounded by identical smaller
versions. She sighs with satisfaction as she finishes writing "SON
FLUOUR AD HIS BABES." Jonathan has completed his drawing; he sits
silently for a few moments, reflectively chewing his pencil. Then he
calls out, "Ms. O'Connell, how do you spell 'this'?"

Few adults looking in on the class would be surprised that children of this age can write and do so enthusiastically. Most adults who
have spent any time at all with young children know that if you
supply paper and writing tools, most children will spontaneously
draw and make writinglike marks. One needs a trained eye, however, to note the wide range of writing and spelling behaviors being
demonstrated by these children. Darleen "writes" using looping
scribbles; Chris writes a continuous line of capital letters without
apparent relation to the sounds of the words he hears in his head.
Roxane also writes in a continuous line without between-word
spaces, but her writing is more readable to others as she begins to use
letters to represent important sounds in the words she chooses. Lolly's
writing is more readable yet, as she uses letters to represent some
of the sounds in her words and also creates spaces between words.
Steven, too, uses between-word spaces and some letter sounds, but
limits his writing to a label rather than a longer production. Jonathan
has drawn but not written anything yet; he has words in mind to use,
but seeks the teacher's help instead of making his own attempt.

All of these children are learning to spell; they are learning what
sounds some of the letters make, and although a few are attempting
to read, none can read easily yet. In this nurturing school environment, these children are functioning as kids who are built to learn to
spell. They are imitating print in their environment. They are inventing printed language. They are interacting with the teacher and other

17

children in a wide range of print-related activities, ranging from shared storybook reading to meaningful and purposeful writing. Within this context, we can say with assurance that they are also learning to spell.

A final important feature of learning to write and spell (as well as to speak) is a willingness to *take risks*; that is, being willing to make mistakes in order to learn, and trusting that the adults around you will support your efforts. Again, children start life with a predisposition to try. If they didn't, none of them would ever get up off all fours and try to walk! Learning to walk is a good example both of children's predisposition to risk failure and of the range of individual differences among children in the factor of risk taking.

What do toddlers do when learning to walk? They fall down a lot! They pull themselves up on a piece of furniture, hold onto it a bit for support, and then finally push off and stagger a few steps. They fall down, right themselves, and try again. They do this over and over, time after time, until they begin to get the hang of it; the balancing, the staggering, the correcting. Their drive to succeed is overwhelming; it simply will not admit defeat. Young children are natural risk takers. They keep trying until they get it right.

Of course, there are great differences among all children. One begins pulling up at eight months, while another crawls or scoots until fifteen months, when Grandma begins to worry if he or she will ever start to walk. One child will use any object for support, even the dog or a visitor's leg, while another will crawl all the way across a room to use the same chair or table each time. One knows no fear, while another is more cautious and plays it safer. Some children are more willing to take risks than others, but all children show us that they are willing to risk failure in order to succeed. And no one, least of all the child, expects them to get it right the first time.

So it must be with learning to write and spell as it is with learning to walk, to talk, to ride a bike, or to eat spaghetti. Many unsuccessful attempts must come before success. We know this, but we often act as if we've forgotten it.

Especially in the area of spelling, we often act as though we can somehow prevent children from making mistakes, and that doing so will help them. Both of these ideas are wrong. If we try to prevent mistakes, we limit children's opportunities to learn. Doing so inhibits, rather than improves, learning. Children must experiment with print, making innumerable mistakes along the way, just as they had to experiment with words and phrases in order to learn to talk, as they had to stumble and fall as they learned to walk, as they have to wobble along and crash before they learn to control a bike. We must not try to prevent spelling errors or react to them as though they are social blunders to be avoided the next time. Inventions and unsuccessful attempts are a natural and inevitable part of learning to spell. Mistakes make it possible for children to spell with success.

Children initially learn to spell by being surrounded with print in their environment, by experimenting with print, and by being willing to risk mistakes in order to eventually get it right. These principles of language learning, which also serve children who are learning to speak, are basic guiding principles for learning to write and spell.

3

Five Stages of Invented Spelling

IN CHAPTER 2 we saw examples of preschoolers and kindergartners who set the foundations for spelling competence by imitating, inventing, interacting, and taking risks in a print-rich environment. As children engage in these activities, they construct or invent a system of spelling. We can identify five successive stages in this system, each qualitatively different from the others and each indicative of a different mind set or cognitive awareness of how spelling works. Each stage represents a critical insight followed by an extension and refinement of understanding about English spelling. Though inventive spellers tend to move in the direction of conventional spelling, the end of this progression is not so much the acquisition of expert spelling ability as a setting of the foundation from which expert spelling might be constructed. In this chapter we will see how the early stages of invented spelling are, for emerging writers and readers, a wonderful and special experience, directly tied to developing three things: familiarity with letters; awareness of phonemes; and knowledge of the alphabetic principle. These three factors serve powerfully to enable spelling and literacy growth.

Early Spelling Acquisition

As we saw in chapter 2, children begin to acquire information about how our spelling system works long before they begin school. They do so as they learn everything else in early childhood: not by being directly taught, but by a process of discovery and experimentation. The key ingredient in this discovery process is experience with print. When young children are read to regularly, when they are shown books and have books to play with and pretend to read, when they see adults writing letters, shopping lists, telephone messages, and other day-to-day kinds of writing, and when they have writing tools and surfaces such as paper, crayons, felt pens, chalk, chalkboards, and sidewalks to play with, they acquire and invent writing spontaneously. When they are denied these early experiences, they may not acquire the information about writing and print they need for later spelling competency.

When a child is read to regularly and frequently, one of the earliest concepts about print he or she acquires is that books and print contain messages that are expressed in words. Books tell stories; magazines have pictures of things, and the things have names; people can write down their words using marks, and others as well as the writer can read the words later. Young children at first do not realize that the stories in books are contained, or encoded, in the print; indeed, at first they respond mostly to the pictures and do not seem to notice the print. Young children often believe that the pictures tell the stories, or that when people read they make up the stories for themselves. Hence, when young prereaders pretend to read to others, they typically turn the pages and name or tell about the pictures on each page, and each successive "reading" of the same book results in a different rendition.

But as they are read the same stories over and over, they discover that the same words are used each time. Have you ever tried to read a child a favorite bedtime story and tried to shorten the reading time by paraphrasing or omitting parts? If so, the child probably interrupted you: "Wait! You left out the part where it says. . . ." At this stage, the young child has discovered that reading a story is *not* making it up as you go along or using just any words to describe what is going on, but is a matter of using the same words each time, in the same order. It is not the story, but the writing that makes this possible.

This may well be the first powerful discovery about print: that it stays the same. And when children's attention is drawn to the print, as well as to the pictures, when they are read to, they begin to notice the printed marks. This opens the door to a number of other powerful

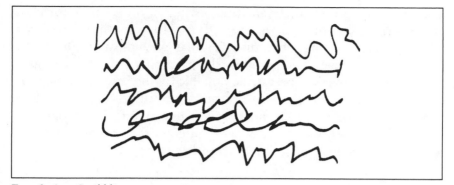

Fig. 3–1   *Scribbling*

discoveries about print and writing. This drawing attention to the print is so easy and natural that many parents and others do it without even realizing what they are doing or why it is so important. All it involves is for the reader to run a finger under the line of print as it is being read. By doing so we show the child where the reader's eyes are during the reading: not on the picture, but on the black marks on the page.

One important discovery children make about writing is that it is arranged horizontally. We know this because linearity, as scholars call it, is the first feature to appear in children's scribbles when they begin to produce different marks for pictures and for writing. At roughly three years of age, children who have had exposure to print in picture books and magazines begin to differentiate between drawing and writing. That is, they begin to use different marks. They draw simple pictures, then use different marks to represent writing. Both the picture and the writing may be mostly scribbles, but the style is different. At the same time, they can begin to point accurately to both the picture and the writing in picture books and magazines, even when the writing is not in English or even when random letters are used.

Children's earliest writing attempts consist of scribbles arranged in horizontal lines. Figure 3–1 shows some examples of this earliest form of writing. The scribbles may be looping or wavy, pointed or curved, but are almost always made of continuous horizontal lines. Children usually do not discover right away that writers move only left to right in English; their attempts may be made in both directions, and many children write one line left to right, then the next in the opposite direction. (Interestingly, the earliest form of Greek writing was made in this way.) But as they continue to be read to and shown writing, they discover that writers of English (and many other languages) write across the page only from left to right. Again, this discovery is best made possible by the reader moving his or her hand under the line of print from left to right, then back again to the left side of the page for the next line. By roughly age four almost all children who have experimented with writing and being read to produce lines of scribbles from left to right.

The Advent of the Alphabetic Principle

As their exposure to print increases, children make another pivotal discovery about print: it is made up not of scribbled marks but of certain kinds of marks. These marks are, of course, the letters of the alphabet, but children do not know this at first. They do discover that the marks have similar features, and a fundamental change occurs when children move away from scribble writing toward character writing. They begin to distinguish the characteristics of written form. At first they may use marks that look something like letters, but are made up of other kinds of characters, as in Figure 3–2. This stage may not last long; indeed, some children seem to skip this stage entirely and move right from scribbles to letters.

When children begin to use letters, they do so at random, for they have not yet discovered the sound-letter relationships that will mark the next major discovery about print. At this stage, however, they have made another powerful discovery: writers do not make up their own writing system; all use the same set of marks, which must be made in roughly the same ways for others to read them. This is the onset of spelling development. It is the first of the five stages of invented spelling: precommunicative, semiphonetic, phonetic, transitional, and conventional. We will look separately at each stage to discover its characteristics and what critical insight the inventive speller must make at each juncture. First, however, let's look at samples of the five stages shown together. Doing so will give us the big picture—a map that charts the progression of the inventive speller from where he or she started to where he or she is going. Table 3–1 presents samples of Leslie's spelling at the precommunicative, semiphonetic, phonetic, transitional, and conventional stages.

24

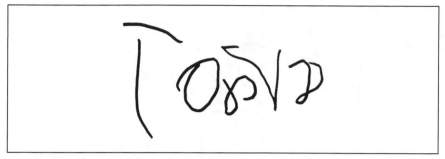

Fig. 3–2   *Character Writing*

TABLE 3–1   Samples of Leslie's Invented Spelling: The Five Stages

Stage	Leslie's Writing	Translation	Age
Precommunicative	EOiiVEiiOE NEMIiEDN MDRMNE	(Story describing a picture of a flock of butterflies)	3 years, 3 months
Semiphonetic (from captions)	ALD GIZ HMT DPD	allowed girls Humpty Dumpty	5 years, 11 months
Phonetic	TAS AS E PACHRR FER MOM I HEP UOU LEK TAS PACHERR EV DNL DEK AND DASY DEC.	This is a picture for Mom. I hope you like this picture of Donald Duck and Daisy Duck.	6 years, 3 months
Transitional	WONES A PON a time we BOTE a LITTEL kitten. You NO how THAY are WHIN THERE little—THERE RASCULES! This one LUVES to CLLIME trees and SRCACH PEPPEL. HE is a MENE RASCULE.		7 years
Conventional	When I went to the zoo, I saw lions. They were sleeping. There were two of them. They were big and HARY.		7 years, 9 months

25

FIG. 3–3   *Precommunicative Spelling: A Grocery List ("Milk, bran flakes, doughnuts")*

The Precommunicative Stage

Figure 3–3 is a sample of precommunicative spelling. The word "precommunicative" is used to describe writing before it can be read by people other than the inventive speller who produced it. The writing represents a message, although it can only be read by the writer and only immediately after it is written. Precommunicative spelling is one result of the learner's discovery of the English letter system. The critical insight developed during precommunicative spelling is familiarity with letters. What the child does *not* know at the precommunicative stage is that letters represent sounds; the alphabetic principle has not been acquired. Development of the critical insight, familiarity with letters, may be enhanced at the precommunicative stage by teaching the visual shapes of letters as well as the names of letters. However, knowledge of letters is probably of little value unless the child knows and is interested in their use. The precommunicative speller can learn a great deal indirectly by meaningful and motivated engagement with print. This knowledge may be greatly extended and refined by the appropriate response of an interested parent or teacher.

Precommunicative spellers are easy to describe (Gentry 1982, 194):

1. They demonstrate some knowledge of the alphabet through production of letter forms to represent a message.
2. They demonstrate no knowledge of letter–sound correspondence. Spelling attempts appear to be a random stringing together of letters of the alphabet that they are able to produce in written form.
3. They may or may not know the principle of left-to-right directionality for English spelling.
4. They may include number symbols as part of the spelling of a word.
5. Their level of alphabet knowledge may range from much repetition of a few known alphabetic symbols to substantial production of many different letters of the alphabet.
6. They frequently mix uppercase and lowercase letters indiscriminately.
7. They generally show a preference for uppercase letter forms.

The emergence of a precommunicative speller is an exciting event; this stage represents the earliest level of spelling.

The Semiphonetic Stage

Figure 3–4 is a sample of semiphonetic spelling. Semiphonetic spellers make a giant cognitive leap from their earlier conceptualization of English orthography at the precommunicative stage: for the first time, they recognize that letters say sounds. This is the critical insight: semiphonetic spelling demonstrates the emergence of the alphabetic principle, the idea that alphabetic letters say sounds. The word "semiphonetic" is used to indicate that the spelling used represents only some of the surface sound features of the word being spelled. Some of the sounds in the word being spelled are either not represented or are not fully spelled phonetically. But it is clear that the semiphonetic speller is beginning to show a second critical insight: an awareness of phonemes, the speech sounds that correspond roughly to individual letters. The recognition that the sounds of

FIG. 3–4   *Semiphonetic Spelling: "Ideas of Quilts"*

syllables can be broken apart and the conscious awareness of the existence of phonemes is an insight, inchoate in the productions of semiphonetic spellers. This knowledge is essential for understanding and using letter-sound correspondences.

The following are characteristic of semiphonetic spellers (Gentry 1982, 195):

1. They begin to conceptualize that letters have sounds that are used to represent sounds in words.
2. They use letters to represent words, but these letters provide a partial, not total, mapping of phonetic representation for the word being spelled. Semiphonetic spelling is abbreviated; one, two, or three letters may be used to represent a larger word.

3. Semiphonetic spellers very often begin their words with initial consonants, which seem to be the easiest to segment. It is not uncommon for semiphonetic writers to represent entire words or syllables by their initial consonants.

4. They very often use letter-name strategies. Where possible, they represent words, sounds, or syllables with letters that match their letter names instead of representing the vowel and consonant sounds separately (examples: R for *are;* U for *you;* LEFT for *elephant*).

5. They have begun to grasp the left-to-right sequential arrangement of letters in English orthography.

6. Their knowledge of the alphabet and mastery of letter formation are becoming more complete.

7. They may or may not be aware of word segmentation.

The evolution to complete phonetic spelling from the early semiphonetic version transpires as semiphonetic spellers enjoy and explore print and actively engage in thinking about words to be written and how best to write them.

The Phonetic Stage

Figure 3–5 is a sample of phonetic spelling. The critical insight gained by the phonetic speller is that all words can be represented phonetically; consequently, phonetic spellers are likely to be prolific writers using a variety of forms: signs, lists, notes, letters, invitations, labels and captions, stories, greeting cards, statements, game boards, and directions. Children's phonetic spelling is the ingenious and systematic invention of an orthographic system that represents all of the sounds they hear in the word being spelled. Phonetic spellers literally spell what they hear. Though some of the phonetic speller's letter choices do not conform to conventional English spelling, the choices are systematic and perceptually correct. Charles Read's (1975) seminal work documents children's phonetic spellings of eighty phone types (sounds), some reflecting obscure details of phonetic form. We will look at some of the most frequently occurring and confusing of the phonetic spellings later in this chapter. Phonetic spellings do not necessarily look like English spelling, but

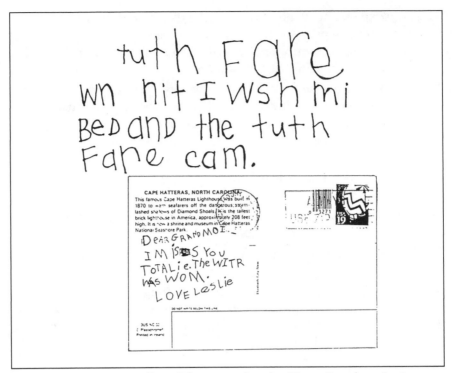

FIG. 3–5   *Phonetic Spelling (The postcard reads, "Dear Grandma, I miss you totally. The water was warm.")*

they are quite readable. Phonetic spellers exhibit the following characteristics (Gentry 1982, 196):

1. For the first time they are able to provide a total mapping of letter-sound correspondence; all of the surface sound features of the words being spelled are represented in the spelling.

2. They systematically develop particular spellings for certain details of phonetic form; namely, tense vowels, lax vowels, preconsonantal nasals, syllabic sonorants, *-ed* endings, retroflex vowels, affricates, and intervocalic flaps (Gentry 1978; Read 1975). These eight sound features are explained more fully in Table 3–2.

3. They assign letters strictly on the basis of sound, without regard for acceptable English letter sequence or other conventions of English orthography.

4. They generally (but not always) show awareness of word segmentation and spatial orientation.

TABLE 3–2   **Eight Sound Features with Unusual Phonetic Spellings**

Sound Feature	What It Means	Sample Word	Phonetic Spelling
Tense vowels	Long vowel sound	eighty	AT (letter name)
		eat	ET
		ice	IC
		oak	OK
		you	U
Lax vowels	Short vowel sound	bat	BUT (vowel shift)
		bet	BAT
		bit	BET
		cot	CIT
		cut	COT
Preconsonantal nasal	*N* or *m* before a consonant	jump	JUP
		stamp	STAP
Syllabic sonorants	I,*m* or *n* carries the vowel sound in a syllable	bottle	BOTL
		atom	ATM
		open	OPN
-Ed endings	Past tense marker	stopped	STOPT
		dimmed	DIMD
		traded	TRADAD
Retroflex vowels	R-controlled vowels	bird	BRD
		sister	SISTR
Affricates	Sounds such as /jr/ and /dr/; /tr/ and /ch/	drag	JRAG
		chip	TRIP
Intervocalic flaps	Sounds made by double *t*'s or *d*'s	bottle	BOTL
		riddle	RIDL

The Transitional Stage

Figure 3–6 is a sample of transitional spelling. Passage into transitional spelling is a remarkable milestone in the journey towards spelling competence. The critical insight of the transitional speller is that he or she must further disassociate written language from spoken language. For the first time, the transitional speller realizes that he or she must write not only what English sounds like but also what

31

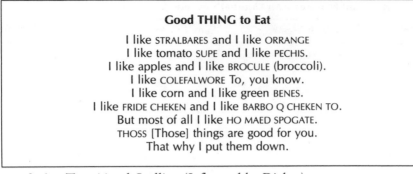

Good THING to Eat

I like STRALBARES and I like ORRANGE
I like tomato SUPE and I like PECHIS.
I like apples and I like BROCULE (broccoli).
I like COLEFALWORE To, you know.
I like corn and I like green BENES.
I like FRIDE CHEKEN and I like BARBO Q CHEKEN TO.
But most of all I like HO MAED SPOGATE.
THOSS [Those] things are good for you.
That why I put them down.

FIG. 3–6   *Transitional Spelling (Influenced by Dialect)*

English *looks* like; consequently, transitional spelling looks very different from the earlier phonetic spelling. For the first time, the inventive speller's productions look like English spelling because the speller is paying attention to what he or she knows about how English looks as well as to what he or she knows about how English sounds. The speller is beginning to recognize that spelling has semantic, historical, and visual demands as well as phonetic ones.

The transitional stage is a time when great integration and differentiation of orthographic forms take place, and it marks a major move toward standard English orthography. During this stage, the speller begins to assimilate the conventional alternatives for representing sounds. The speller undergoes a transition from great reliance on sound for representing words in the printed form to much greater reliance on visual and morphological representations. During this stage, instruction in reading and spelling facilitates the move toward spelling competence, but the changes affecting the speller's conceptualization of orthography may be too complex to be explained by a simple visual memorization of spelling patterns (Chomsky and Halle 1968; Gentry 1982; Henderson and Beers 1980; Read and Hodges 1983).

Transitional spellers are characterized as follows (Gentry 1982, 197):

1. They adhere to basic conventions of English orthography: vowels appear in every syllable (e.g., EGUL instead of the phonetic EGL for *eagle*); nasals are represented before consonants (e.g., BANGK instead of the phonetic BAK for *bank*); both vowels and consonants are employed instead of a letter-name strategy (e.g., EL rather than

32

L for the first syllable of *elephant*); a vowel is represented before syllabic *r* even though it is not heard or felt as a separate sound (e.g., MONSTUR instead of the phonetic MOSTR for *monster*); common English letter sequences are used in spelling (e.g., YOUNITED for *united*, STINGKS for *stinks*); especially liberal use of vowel digraphs like *ai;* combinations such as *ea, ay, ee,* and *ow* appear; the silent *e* becomes fixed as an alternative for spelling long vowel sounds (e.g., TIPE in place of the phonetic TIP for *type*); and inflectional endings like *-s, -'s, -ing,* and *-est* are spelled conventionally.

2. Transitional spellers present the first evidence of a new visual strategy; they move from phonological to morphological and visual spelling (e.g., EIGHTEE instead of the phonetic ATE for *eighty*).

3. Because of this new visual strategy, transitional spellers may include all appropriate letters, but they may reverse some letters (e.g., TAOD for *toad,* HUOSE for *house,* OPNE for *open*). Perhaps this phenomenon is due to interference, as a lot of new information is being processed concurrently. The new visual strategy, though in use, is not yet integrated to the point that the speller recognizes what looks right.

4. Transitional spellers have not fully developed the use of factors identified by researchers that contribute to spelling competence: graphemic environment of the unit, position in the word, stress, morpheme boundaries, and phonological influences (Bissex 1980; Gibson and Levin 1975; Venezky 1970).

5. Transitional spellers differentiate alternate spellings for the same sound. A long *a* sound, for example, may be spelled the following ways by a transitional speller: EIGHTE (eighty), ABUL (able), LASEE (lazy), RANE (rain), and SAIL (sale). However, as indicated in item 4 above, the conditions governing particular alternatives for representing a sound are only partially understood at the transitional stage.

6. Transitional spellers generally use learned words (correctly spelled words) in greater abundance in their writing. Beyond the transitional stage, children typically spell with increasingly greater accuracy, especially if their use of words in writing is coupled with spelling instruction.

The Conventional Stage

The transitional stage is one of the most important stages of invented spelling because it signals readiness for more direct spelling instruction. That is, transitional spellers enter a developmental phase in which they need opportunities to look at words in specific and intent ways in order to internalize visual, and later semantic and etymological, patterns. Thus begins the process of formal spelling instruction. How to make the important move from invented spelling into more formal instruction initiated during the transitional stage is discussed in detail in chapter 5 and in subsequent chapters. In fact, conventional spelling is usually viewed from the instructional scheme rather than the developmental scheme. We can roughly gauge the level of conventional spelling accomplishment by the number of frequently occurring words that are spelled accurately. For example, a "third grade level speller" is one who spells with accuracy the corpus of frequently occuring words that a majority of third graders who are developmentally on target have mastered. Likewise, a sixth grade level speller has mastered the frequently occurring words that the typical sixth grader can spell. Word lists for measuring levels of conventional spelling, which are discussed in chapter 5, are generated from cross-sectional word frequency studies of spelling accuracy in children's writing. Some studies indicate that seventh graders average 95 percent accuracy for spelling on essays (Jongsma 1990). At first glance 95 percent accuracy might sound like good conventional spelling, but in fact, misspelling five words of every hundred words written is catastrophic for mature spellers. Expert conventional spelling requires time, instruction, and effort. Conventional spellers develop over years of word study, reading, and writing.

Perhaps there isn't just one critical insight for conventional spelling, but rather integration of several. Conventional spellers know the English orthographic system and how it works. They are able to integrate and process the semantic, etymological, and visual demands as well as the phonetic demands of the system. More experience with words and more formal instruction further refine and extend the orthographic knowledge of the conventional speller. Conventional spelling is, in fact, a lifelong process.

Here are the characteristics of conventional spellers (Gentry 1982, 198):

1. Their knowledge of the English orthographic system and its basic rules is firmly established.

2. They extend their phonetic knowledge, including knowledge of spelling for word environmental constraints (i.e., graphemic environment in the word, position in word, and stress).

3. They show an extended knowledge of semantic demands and word structure, including accurate spelling of prefixes, suffixes, contractions, and compound words, and an ability to distinguish homonyms.

4. They demonstrate growing accuracy in using silent consonants and in doubling consonants appropriately.

5. They are able to think of alternative spellings and employ visual identification of misspelled words as a correction strategy (in other words, they know when words don't look right).

6. They continue to master uncommon alternative patterns (e.g., *ie* and *ei*) and words with irregular spellings.

7. They have mastered etymological demands such as Latinate forms and other etymological structures that reflect the word's sources.

8. They have accumulated a large corpus of learned words.

This overview of the five stages of invented spelling shows that spelling development is constructive and continuous and proceeds from simple to complex and from concrete to more abstract form. In chapter 5 we will see that what makes an expert speller is the internalization of this complex system, with the integration of phonetic, semantic, etymological, and visual knowledge in an interactive process. These different types of knowledge likely are processed in parallel. In order for a person to become a conventional speller, he or she must acquire a great deal of phonetic, semantic, etymological, and visual knowledge about words and must then activate this knowledge in a complex cognitive process.

Recognizing Phonetic Spelling

The technical terminology that accompanies any in-depth discussion of invented spelling can be mind-boggling. Terms such as "preconsonantal nasals," "affricates," and "labial stops" have little meaning for most readers. Such terminology makes understanding the stages of invented spelling seem complex. It's not. The stage most teachers or parents have some difficulty identifying is phonetic. Phonetic spellings are unfamiliar; they look different from what most of us expect. To help you better grasp phonetic spelling, try this: For a few moments imagine that the only information you have about how to spell words is phonetic. Pick up a pencil with the perspective of a six-year-old phonetic speller. Now follow the instructions in the following list. Remember, as a phonetic speller you must first decide what sounds you hear in a word. Then you must write down a letter for each sound. This activity will take you through a thought process similar to the one used by a six-year-old phonetic speller. (Answers are given at the end of the chapter.)

1. Phonetic spellers often spell the short vowel sound with an incorrect vowel. Spell the following words as if you were a phonetic speller. Choose a vowel that sounds like the sound that you hear in the middle of the word:

Word	Your Phonetic Spelling
pet	P __ T
bit	B __ T
hot	H __ T
hut	H __ T

2. Phonetic spellers systematically omit *n* and *m* (which make the nasal sounds) when they occur before consonants. Spell the following words.

Word	Your Phonetic Spelling
monster	__ __ __ __ __
stamp	__ __ __ __
sing	__ __ __
jumping	__ __ __ __ __

3. Phonetic spellers omit the vowel when the syllable has a consonant that carries the vowel sound. Spell the following words.

Word	Phonetic Spelling
open	__ __ __
bottle	__ __ __ __
sister	__ __ __ __ __
bird	__ __ __

4. Phonetic spellers mix up some consonant blends that are formed the same way when we articulate them. Two phonetic spellings are presented below. Can you provide the correct spelling?

Phonetic Spelling	Conventional Spelling
JRAGN	_____
CHUK	_____

5. Phonetic spellers may spell the *-ed* ending three different ways. Spell it below.

Word	Phonetic Spelling
peeked	PEK ____
dimmed	DIM ____
baited	BAT ____ ____

Once you understand the nuances of phonetic spelling, it is not difficult to recognize the stages of invented spelling. If you simply observe children's invented spelling and think about what they were thinking when they invented it, you're already on your way to becoming an expert at analyzing invented spelling.

Answers:
1. PAT, BET, HIT, HOT
2. MOSTR, STAP, SEG, JOPEG
3. OPN, BOTL, SISTR, BRD
4. DRAGON, TRUCK
5. PEKT, DIMD, BATAD

4

Assessing Invented
Spelling:
Snapshots of the Mind

EACH TIME A child or adult invents a spelling, he or she produces
a telling snapshot of how the mind conceives of spelling. Each
invented spelling is a permanent record of an individual's journey to
spelling competence. If we collect these snapshots, these invented
spellings, and analyze them, we can put together a remarkable album
that shows milestones along the way. Since the journey unfolds
developmentally in patterns that are predictable and systematic, we
can chart the journey with precision and accuracy.

Our view of invented spellings as snapshots of the mind does not
mean we have lost sight of the complexity of spelling as a visual and
cognitive process. But we can "see" a lot of what is going on in the
speller's mind if we know how to analyze invented spelling from a
developmental perspective.

In chapter 3 you learned how to identify five different stages of
invented spelling: precommunicative, semiphonetic, phonetic, transitional, and conventional. In this chapter we will use that information to assess early development.

Studying Spelling Changes

At the beginning of first grade Ted was reluctant to write and was
confused about spelling. Towards the end of the year, in May,
his teacher, Mrs. Bateman, used two writing samples from Ted's

writing folder to show his parents how he was overcoming his reluctance to write and gaining in spelling confidence.

First, Mrs. Bateman showed Ted's parents a story Ted had written in early January:

WNS THEIR WUZ a MRSHN and a man CAM TO SPAS. THE MRSHN had a SPAS GN. He BLU up a STR. The man BLU up the MRSHN. That was the ND of the MRSHN.	Once there was a Martian and a man came to space. The Martian had a space gun. He blew up a star. The man blew up the Martian. That was the end of the Martian.

Mrs. Bateman then explained the significance of Ted's writing to his parents. "I can show you that Ted is making developmental gains in spelling by pointing out changes in his invented spelling in two writing samples: the first written in January, the second written in May," she began. "In January Ted was a phonetic speller. He didn't know what English spelling was supposed to look like, but he successfully invented spellings by choosing a letter to match each sound or phoneme he heard in a word. In January Ted could segment four sounds in the word *space*: /s/, /p/, /ā/, and /s/. This ability to break down the sounds in words is important for beginning readers and writers. Ted's spelling strategy in January was to write a letter to represent each sound. For *space* he wrote S for /s/, P for /p/, A for /ā/, and S for /s/. SPAS was a good try for a phonetic speller using a strategy that mapped letters directly to sounds. Now let's look at Ted's invented spellings in May." She showed them the following story:

My COINES

I have a 1964 dime and QURTER. They are PRUE SLIVER. I got one from my TECHER and one from my dad. They are WERTH A BOUT 3 DOLERS ECH. I have PENIES, NIKLES, dimes and QURTERS. I like TINE COINES.

Mrs. Bateman continued, saying, "Ted's strategy for spelling has changed. By May, Ted not only thought about how words sounded when he spelled them, he also thought about how they were supposed to look. He knew English words met certain visual conventions. His invented spellings were much more sophisticated in May as he drew from what he knew about frequent English letter sequences, spellings for endings like -ed and -es, use of vowels in syllables, e-markers, and consonant and vowel digraphs. These samples clearly show a change. In January Ted didn't have vowels in every syllable, but look, he consistently included vowels in every syllable in May:

/Kw/ /o/ /r/ /t/ /r/
Q   U R T ER

"Furthermore," she continued, "Ted abandoned January spellings such as WNS (once), MRSHN (Martian) and GN (gun) for much more sophisticated spellings that include e-markers and vowels in every syllable. He would probably have spelled these words ONSE, MARSHUN, and GON in May. This is a powerful signal of his positive growth in spelling. In the May sample Ted is processing spelling at a higher level. He has moved closer to conventional spelling. For the first time he is picturing words in his mind when he spells them, and he is applying conventions that he has discovered about how English spelling looks. It doesn't matter that Ted made fourteen spelling errors when he wrote 'My Coins'; as you can see, he is making remarkable progress as a speller."

Because Ted's teacher knew how to watch for changes in invented spelling, she was able to assess his developmental growth and point out to Ted's parents qualitative changes in his invented spellings. Mrs. Bateman then explained how the changes represented progress. Her ability to recognize the developmental changes found in the two pieces written five months apart was a powerful tool for assessment. It would help her plan for instruction and measure growth. It enabled her to show how Ted had constructed new knowledge about spelling in the last five months of first grade.

The Developmental Spelling Test

All teachers, particularly teachers in kindergarten and first and second grades, need to watch for changes in invented spelling. To help with this task, we have designed a developmental spelling test to help teachers determine the specific stage of development at which a child is functioning at a particular point. Invented spellings may be analyzed in the context of children's writing, using the developmental spelling test has advantages: it is controlled, quick to administer, easy to analyze, and generally provides the same results as painstaking analysis of numerous invented spellings taken from lengthy samples of a child's writing. The developmental spelling test is a simple analysis of ten words; the idea is to determine what percentage of the words were spelled with precommunicative, semiphonetic, phonetic, transitional, or conventional strategies. A majority of the spellings in one category designates the speller's likely developmental level.

Administer the test

Administer the developmental spelling test printed below to a five-, six-, or seven-year-old. The test is designed for pupils in kindergarten through second grade. When you administer the list, you will obtain spellings that can be categorized roughly into five developmental stages: precommunicative, semiphonetic, phonetic, transitional, and conventional. Once you have analyzed one or two tests, you will be an expert at noticing the same patterns of spelling in young children's free writing.

Here are the directions. Call out each word; give the sentence provided; and call out the word again. Explain that the words may be too difficult for most kindergartners and first graders to spell. What you want your pupils to do is invent the spelling or use their best guess at what the spelling might be. Explain that the activity will not be graded as right or wrong, but will be used to see how children think certain difficult words should be spelled. Be encouraging, and make the activity challenging, playful, and fun.

Here are the ten words in the test:

1. **monster**   The boy was eaten by a monster.
2. **united**   You live in the United States.
3. **dress**   The girl wore a new dress.
4. **bottom**   A big fish lives at the bottom of the lake.
5. **hiked**   We hiked to the top of the mountain.
6. **human**   Miss Piggy is not a human.
7. **eagle**   An eagle is a powerful bird.
8. **closed**   The little girl closed the door.

9. bumped   The car bumped into the bus.

10. type   Type the letter on the typewriter.

Analyze the spellings

Table 4–1 will help you analyze the spellings. Before going further, think about the features that you will look for at each developmental level.

1. *Precommunicative spelling* is the "babbling" stage of spelling. Children use letters for writing words, but the letters are strung together randomly. The letters in precommunicative spelling do not correspond to sounds. Look for spellings such as OPSPS for *eagle* or RTES for *monster*.

2. *Semiphonetic spellers* know that letters represent sounds. They perceive and reliably represent sounds with letters in a type of telegraphic writing. Spellings are often abbreviated, representing initial and/or final sounds. For example, E for *eagle* and M for *monster* are semiphonetic spellings. Only some of many possible semiphonetic combinations are represented in Table 4–1.

3. *Phonetic spellers* spell words like they sound. The speller perceives and represents all of the phonemes in a word, though spellings may be unconventional. EGL for *eagle* and BOTM for *bottom* are good examples of phonetic spelling.

4. *Transitional spellers* think about how words appear visually; a visual memory of spelling patterns is apparent. Spellings exhibit conventions of English orthography, such as vowels in every syllable, *e*-marker and vowel digraph patterns, correctly spelled inflectional endings, and frequent English letter sequences. Transitional examples include EGUL for *eagle* and BOTTUM for *bottom*. To distinguish between phonetic spellings (influenced by sound) and transitional spellings (influenced by visual conventions), ask the question: Was this word spelled like it sounds (phonetic) or is its spelling analogous to a visually recalled spelling (transitional)?

5. *Conventional spellers* develop over years of word study and writing. Conventional spelling can be categorized by instructional

levels; for example, correct spelling of a general corpus of commonly used words that can be spelled by the average fourth grader would be fourth grade level conventional spelling. Place a given test response in this category if the word is spelled correctly. In words of more than one syllable, if one syllable is spelled at one level and another syllable at a different level, classify the word at the lower developmental level.

Now look at the child's spelling for each word in the developmental spelling test. Find the error type in Table 4–1 that best matches the child's spelling. Write the appropriate developmental label (precommunicative, semiphonetic, phonetic, transitional, or conventional) beside each of the ten spellings. Where most of the child's spellings fall is the child's probable developmental level.

Even though ten words is a small sample, this test will reveal the types of developmental errors that a child is likely to make when free writing. Observe invented spellings in the child's free writing to verify the child's level of development. Remember that many of the child's spellings in free writing may be correct. Children who are at lower developmental levels may have memorized spellings for words like *cat*. Children's *misspellings* are what provide snapshots of their minds to reveal their developmental level.

Now you are ready to use what you know about invented spelling. Can you read the adaptation of "The Three Little Pigs" written by a six-year-old first grader and shown in Figure 4–1?

TABLE 4–1   Possible Test Responses

Word	Precommunicative	Semiphonetic	Phonetic	Transitional	Conventional
1. monster	random letters	MTR	MOSTR	MONSTUR	monster
2. united	random letters	U	UNITD	YOUNIGHTED	united
3. dress	random letters	JRS	JRAS	DRES	dress
4. bottom	random letters	BT	BODM	BOTTUM	bottom
5. hiked	random letters	H	HIKT	HICKED	hiked
6. human	random letters	UM	HUMN	HUMUN	human
7. eagle	random letters	EL	EGL	EGUL	eagle
8. closed	random letters	KD	KLOSD	CLOSSED	closed
9. bumped	random letters	B	BOPT	BUMPPED	bumped
10. type	random letters	TP	TIP	TIPE	type

Source: Adapted from Gentry 1985.

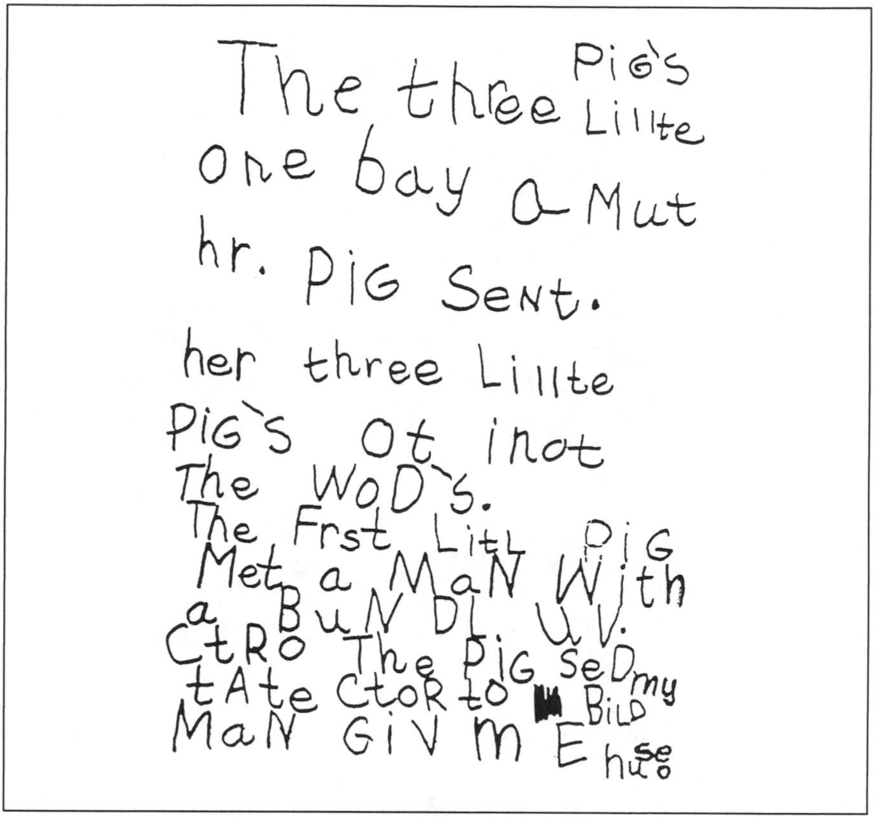

The three Pig's Lillte
one bay a Mut
hr. PiG SeNt.
her three Lillte
PiG's Ot inot
The WoD's.
The Frst Litl PiG
Met a MaN With
a BuNDl UV.
CtRO The PiG SeD my
tAte CtoR to BiLD
MaN GiV mE hus

FIG. 4–1   *Adaptation of "The Three Little Pigs"*

This sample may be a challenge for you, especially the ending. Beginning writers often follow the old adage "necessity is the mother of invention" as they space, spell, and punctuate. The six-year-old who wrote this story ran out of space at the end of the page. Insistent that the whole story should fit on one page, she simply squeezed the words in wherever they would fit. Be prepared to experience similar kinds of experimentation and risk taking with the spacing, spelling, and punctuation of beginning writers. Remember, they still have lots of discoveries to make.

Now, try reading "The Three Little Pigs" again. This time we've cut it up and pieced it back together to help you decipher it (Figure 4–2).

Now that you have read and enjoyed the story, it's time to ask a question of secondary importance: At what level of development is

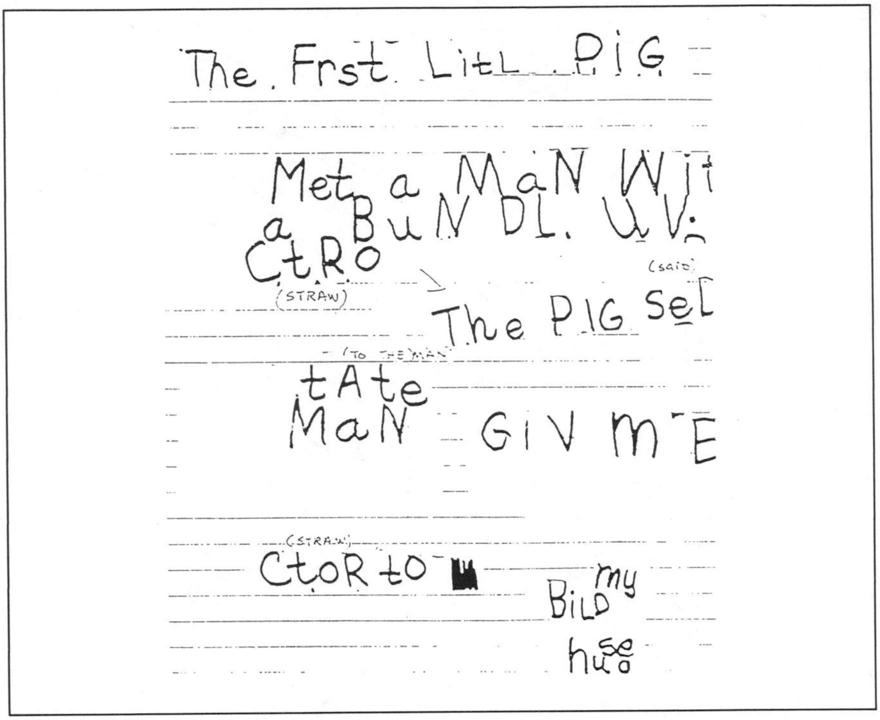

The. Frst. LitL. PIG

Met a MaN Wit
a BuNDL. UV.
CtRO
(STRAW)
The PIG SeL
(said)
(TO THE MAN)
tAte
MaN GIV mE

(STRAW)
CtoR tO
BiLD my
huSe

FIG. 4–2   *"The Three Little Pigs" in More Conventional Order*

this inventive speller functioning? We could analyze the seventeen invented spellings in "The Three Little Pigs," but a much more controlled, convenient, and easy way to analyze her spelling is to administer the developmental spelling test. Figure 4–3 presents our six-year-old's invented spellings for the word list. (She wrote "The Three Little Pigs" and took the developmental spelling test on the same day.) Let's walk through an analysis of the spelling list word by word. Remember, *phonetic* is spelling by sound, *transitional* is spelling by sight:

1. MONSTR (*monster*) is a bit tricky to classify. MON is a conventional spelling of the first syllable, but STR, with no vowel, is phonetic. Since phonetic is the lower level, let's classify MONSTR as phonetic.

2. UNITD (*united*) represents all the surface sounds of the word. It's in Table 4–1. Classify UNITD as phonetic.

46

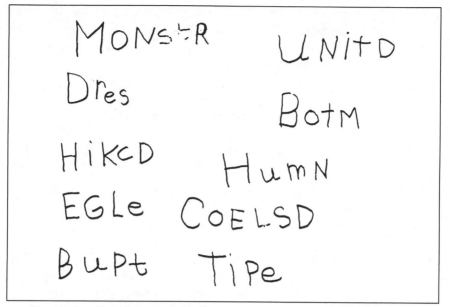

FIG. 4–3   *Developmental Spelling Test*

3. DRES (*dress*) is a transitional spelling (as shown in Table 4–1). It looks a lot like conventional English spelling.

4. BOTM (*bottom*) is spelled as it sounds. It doesn't look like English, but all of the sounds are represented. Classify BOTM as phonetic.

5. HIKCD (*hiked*) has all the sounds represented, but it doesn't look like English spelling; it is classified as phonetic.

6. HUMN (*human*) is spelled as it sounds. Classify HUMN as phonetic.

7. EGLE (*eagle*) has vowels in every syllable and looks much like English spelling; classify it transitional. (EGL would be phonetic, but EGLE is more sophisticated, since it uses -*le* at the end of the word, an easily recognized visual pattern.)

8. COELSD (*closed*) is difficult to classify. All six letters in *closed* were used, so it may be transitional. But the letters are scrambled, and some are far from appropriate within-word placement. We would rate this spelling as unclassifiable.

9. BUPT (*bumped*) has a nasal /m/ sound before a consonant, which phonetic spellers systematically leave out. They are in fact spelling by sound. The *-ed* ending is spelled T like it sounds, not like it looks. Classify BUPT as phonetic.

10. TIPE (*type*) with its visually inspired *e*-marker pattern is recognized as a transitional spelling (see Table 4–1).

Here's a quick tabulation of the six-year-old's invented spelling:

- 60 percent phonetic.
- 30 percent transitional.
- 10 percent unclassifiable.

These results indicate that this six-year-old first grader is a phonetic speller who is just beginning to use some transitional strategies. If you were to analyze the invented spellings in her "Three Little Pigs" story you would discover the same developmental level of functioning: thirteen phonetic spellings and four transitional spellings. In both story and test she uses the same strategies, the same pattern for spelling. This is a powerful discovery for a teacher. As you will see in the next chapter, knowing her level would enable you to engage this budding writer in developmentally appropriate activities designed to facilitate her growth. You would be able to look at her invented spellings three months hence and determine spelling development or stagnation. You could show parents exactly how she is progressing. You could unlock the next gate or point her in the right direction as she journeys onward down her personal path to literacy—a journey that leads her to new worlds, to a richer and fuller life.

What Makes an Expert Speller:

The Phonetic, Semantic, Historical, and Visual Demands

WE HAVE SEEN how the early stages of invented spelling unfold naturally, much like the acquisition of speech. In time, however, learning to spell becomes harder than learning to speak. The demands of spelling are intensified when inventive spellers realize that spellings must account not only for how words sound but also for how they look. Later spellers recognize the semantic and etymological requirements of spelling. Inventive spellers must ultimately disassociate written language from spoken language in order to spell correctly. In the final analysis, expert spelling involves looking at words intensely and in specific ways and making phonetic, semantic, etymological, and visual associations in order to learn to spell them. What makes an expert speller is the internalization of a complex system with phonetic, semantic, historical, and visual knowledge of words processed interactively and in parallel. Optimal operation of the system likely depends on receiving accurate and timely input and on processing a well-integrated response to the input.

The Phonetic Demand

Because English is an alphabetic writing system, the phonetic demand of the system is obvious: sounds must correspond to letters. The problem is that there is no direct one-to-one correspondence of sounds to letters in English. All spellers of English must "escape the tyranny of sound" (Cummings 1988, p. 14). This is as true today for a five- or six-year-old inventive speller who is learning the system for the first time as it was for the Christian monks in England who invented English spelling during the early Middle Ages. They, too, struggled with the tyranny of sound when they began to write down Old English in their modified Latin alphabet. Inventive spellers, whoever they are, have to begin by relating letters to the sounds being spoken. They begin by relying on the ear (Cummings 1988) and, in doing so, come up with different spellings for the same words. In Old and Middle English the phonetic demand was in sole control. *Husband,* for example, had over thirty spellings, including *husbonde, husebande, husebonde, hosebaunde, hosband, housbond, hosbon, huszbande, housbande, hisband,* and *housebounde* (Cummings 1988, p. 21).

The spelling of fourteenth-century Middle English was fraught with whimsy and confusion due to the sole control of the phonetic demand and the variance of sounds in different dialects. Spelling was a mess! Recognition of this problem led to the standardization and use of Chancery English in fifteenth-century Westminster. This marked the advent of standard written English as we know it today (Fisher 1977; Samuels 1963) and the introduction of the semantic, etymological, and visual demands of spelling.

The Semantic Demand

The semantic demand dictates that a given semantic or meaning unit be spelled consistently from word to word. For example, *sign,* a meaning unit, is always spelled *s-i-g-n* even though it has four different sounds:

- *sign* |sin| (rhymes with *dine*)
- *sign*al |sig| + |n| (rhymes with *dig* + n)
- de*sign* |zin| (sounds like the first part of *Zion*)
- de*sign*ate |zig| + n   (sounds like the first part of *Ziggy*)

Much knowledge about the semantic demand is learned by reading and writing. Many maturing readers and writers (beginning at about age eleven) come to realize the semantic connection between words like *nation* and *national,* which have similar spellings because of the similarity in meaning, not pronunciation. For older children, semantic relationships among words are one of the important organizing principles for spelling instruction (Templeton 1979).

The Historical Demand

The historical demand, which often parallels the semantic, is that a word's spelling reflect its etymology or history. In addition to a semantic demand, *sign* carries a historical demand relating it to the Latin *signum*. Another example is the *ll* in *llama*. Although initial *ll* is rare in English, the word, relatively recently adopted from Spanish, meets the historical demand and retains its original Spanish spelling.

The Visual Demand

The visual demand has increased with the growing importance of print and silent reading, both relatively recent language developments. The number of acceptable variant spellings in modern English is on the decline. In its place is a strong bias for visual conformity, which will increase even more as technology brings world communications systems closer together.

How important is visualization for spelling? The answer is revealed by a relatively simple test. We call it the "carrot test." Here it is. Try your hand at it. (Answers provided in the text that follows.)

Directions: In the space provided, spell each word as defined and used in the sentence.

1. _____ a unit for measuring the fineness of gold. (The watch is made of 24 ——— gold.)

2. _____ a unit of weight in gemstones equal to 200 milligrams. (She wore a two ——— diamond.)

3. _____ an orange edible root. (The rabbit nibbled on the ———.)

4. _____ a mark used to insert something in text. (Use a ——— to indicate where to add the phrase to the sentence.)

Now think about what strategy you used to spell the words. What were you thinking as you chose the letters for each of the four spellings? Was spelling a problem for you, or did each of the spellings

51

come easily? Did some words come more easily than others? Why do you think that was so?

Now think generally. What is your strategy for spelling *any* word when the spelling for the word is not automatic?

Expert spellers internalize the spellings of more and more words as they mature. Knowing words by heart or spelling them automatically seems to be closely related to how well an individual can store and retrieve the visual form of a word. Visualization of words plays a large part in determining spelling accuracy.

Expert Spellers and Poor Spellers Do Not Spell Alike

Expert spellers visualize words. They have an ability to store and retrieve the visual form of the word in their brain. These spellers seem literally to see the word in their mind's eye. If you could spell most of the words on the carrot test, you drew from associative linkages perhaps relating phonetic, semantic, etymological, and visual knowledge. But at some point you probably constructed the visual form of the word in your mind's eye. You retrieved an image of what the word looks like. Most poor spellers cannot do that. Their brain apparently functions differently. They do not seem to have a fully functional ability to store and retrieve the visual form of the word. This visual coding mechanism may be analogous to the ability to carry a tune: there is no evidence it can be taught. Expert spellers may, in fact, be born, not made; the visual coding mechanism may be attributed to inborn brain organization.

Poor spellers do not demonstrate equal ability to store and retrieve the visual form of a word; so they may revert to a lower-level strategy. When asked to spell an unfamiliar word, they spell it like it sounds, not unlike the lower-level phonetic strategy of inventive spellers. As you can see, this strategy isn't very efficient or effective with English, especially when you are trying to spell words such as *karat, carat, carrot,* and *caret* (which happen to be the correct order of answers to our carrot test). They all sound exactly alike! Why are some of us good at spelling and some not? It may be because some of us have the ability to store and retrieve the visual form of the word; some of us "see" *karat* when thinking of the word for 24-karat gold; some "see" *carat* when thinking of the word for measuring weight in gemstones. Others of us cannot effectively visualize the words in our mind's eye. Unfortunately, how the brain works for spelling is not yet well enough understood for us to explain *why* some of us can store and retrieve visual word forms while others can't. For the time being, we can only state that this condition exists.

The Relationship of Expert Spelling to Intelligence

If there is a relationship between expert spelling and intelligence, it would seem from casual observation to be the opposite from what one might expect. The fact is that many extremely intelligent or gifted people can*not* spell. One might conclude, from casual observation, that poor spelling is a sign of superior intelligence! Perhaps we're being hyperbolic, but you get the point: superior intelligence is not indicative of expert spelling ability. If you're an expert speller, it's not because of your great intelligence.

Poor spellers are often heartened by the revelation that people of high achievement may be lousy spellers. George Washington couldn't spell well. Neither could Thomas Edison or Albert Einstein or Auguste Rodin. Cher can't spell; neither can Tom Cruise. George Bush isn't very good at it. Andrew Jackson was a pitiful speller who once said, "It's a damn poor mind that can think of only one way to spell a word!" Don't feel too bad about yourself if you can't spell; maybe you just weren't born with a fully functional visual coding mechanism.

Remarkable Misspellings

The kinds of errors that poor spellers struggle with, even those who are conscientious and work at improving their poor spelling, may seem rather remarkable to expert spellers. If you are a poor speller, you may feel as if you are the only one who experiences these rather bizarre spelling inadequacies. Let's take a look at some typical errors of spellers whose visual coding mechanism is not fully functional.

Inability to recall spellings of commonly used words

Some poor spellers consistently misspell certain demon words. One good example is the word *before*. Is it *befor* or *before*? What makes this one particularly confusing are associations such as *forehead, four, forty, fourteen,* and *for.* Don't try to figure it out logically. If *four* is the number, why not *fourty?* If *f-o-r* works for *forty* why not *forteen?* Words with the *f-o-r, f-o-u-r, f-o-r-e* letter combinations, which include ill-formed spellings such as *forty,* can drive spellers without a strong visual coding mechanism crazy!

Inability to recall studied and learned spellings

A speller without a fully functional visual coding mechanism can learn the correct spelling of an unfamiliar word such as *paradigm,* use the word over and over in an article written about *paradigms,* then not think about or have occasion to write the word for three or four weeks, and discover that he or she has forgotten how to spell it. Three weeks later, if the word is needed, it might just as likely be spelled *paradymn!*

Inability to see misspellings

Spellers without a functional visual coding mechanism often spell a word two different ways in the same paper, proofread the paper over and over, and still never see the different spellings. For example, the word *enigmatic* may be spelled *enigmantic* on one page and *inegmatic* on the next; yet the poor speller who proofreads the pages would never notice the difference even after two or three careful readings.

The point is rather poignant (or is it *poinent?*); many people simply do not have a nack (*knack?*) for storing and retrieving the visual form of a spelling. When called upon to spell a word, expert spellers can see it, but poor spellers can't. One of the tasks of teachers is to use instructional techniques designed to improve children's abilities to visually store and retrieve words.

Children Who Cannot Store and Retrieve Visual Spellings

The visual coding mechanism is elusive and complex. It is not simple visual memory or a learning style. Undoubtedly, it works in parallel with other processing mechanisms related to spelling. Certainly phonemic, semantic, and etymological associative linkages function in parallel with it, allowing the mind to consider input on different levels and to look for overlap and connections. We cannot fully explain how the visual coding mechanism works, but we can show you what spelling can look like in children for whom it is not fully functional.

For all practical purposes, twelve-year-old Kelly should be an excellent speller. She is very bright, she loves to read, and she is, in fact, a voracious reader. For reasons no one understands, she entered seventh grade with a crippling and agonizing history of spelling disability. (Perhaps not surprisingly, her father, an engineer, also suffers from being a poor speller. Her brilliant older brother, though, is an expert speller.) Kelly had not learned to spell by reading. Her extremely poor spelling had resulted in poor grades, family crises, and an assault on her self-esteem. Poor spelling was causing her to be a reluctant and not-very-successful writer. When Kelly began seventh grade, her writing samples usually exhibited spelling at 93 percent accuracy; 95 percent is considered average at the seventh-grade level (Jongsma 1990). Nonetheless, her spelling was a catastrophe, as the following example demonstrates:

> I am twelve years old! I love horses. I live in the woods right next TWO my GRARDFATHERS farm. In the summer I go to camp where I care for and ride horses. I like COLITING horses (figurines). I'm in 4-H. I have 3 sheep, 2 horses, and 3 cows. One of my favorite things is to take long walks all over the farm. I also love reading books. My FAVORERES are *The BLALK Stallion, HIEDY,* and *The Call of the Wild.*

Five of the six words Kelly misspelled—*to, grandfather, collecting, favorites,* and *black*—are words she had previously mastered for spelling tests. *To* and *black* are commonly used first grade level words. The sixth word, *Heidi,* is a word Kelly has seen literally hundreds of times in reading and rereading her favorite book. Kelly's spelling illustrates a partially malfunctioning visual coding mechanism.

Stacy's situation is remarkably similar. Also twelve years old, Stacy is bright, she makes good grades, and she is a natural and excellent reader. She has always been a poor speller, but it hasn't been devastating to her because she has always been a favorite of her teachers. The following letter to her uncle reveals unusual spellings similar to Kelly's, explicable only by consideration of a partially functional visual coding mechanism:

Dear Uncle Richard,

Thank you so much for the trip to Atlanta. I'm very lucky to have you as my uncle. You do a lot for me and I appreciate the things you do.

You and Carol are fun to be around. You guy's thought of great places to go like the Swan House and UNDER GROUND. I loved that one—you know—where we ate Mexican food and Carol told the waiter he was SEXEST. I learned a lot from Carol, but don't worry.

Well, I started school. Math is not my subject. BOC [block] Studies is. My teacher is great. Her name is Miss Hubbard. She has this way of teaching you. I make all A's in her class.

Well, got to go. See YA at the dinner table for turkey and stuffing.

Love,
Stacy G.

P.S. I want long hair! I had to say SONTHING NAGITIVE. My TOUNG would have FALLEN out. BUY.

Apparently Stacy's P.S. was a quick, whimsical afterthought, perhaps written on the spur of the moment, frivolously and hastily and consequently with a surge of invented spelling. At that moment, was Stacy's visual coding mechanism, ordinarily partially functioning, completely shut off?

In addition to reading and writing daily in a language-rich environment, children must be taught phonetic, semantic, etymological, and visual knowledge of words both directly and indirectly in order to internalize them and use them interactively for producing correct spelling. In the chapters ahead we will explore instructional models and individual activities to help children meet the phonetic, semantic, historical, and visual demands of spelling.

6

A Workshop Approach to Teaching Spelling

SPELLING IS A tool for writing. The purpose of learning to spell is so that writing may become easier, more fluent, more expressive, and more easily read and understood by others. Without writing, there would be little purpose in learning to spell. Thus, the proper place for spelling instruction is within the writing program. Active daily writing, for real purposes and real audiences, is necessary for spelling development in all grades. The first part of this chapter discusses the role of spelling in the writing program.

However, for many students active writing is not enough. Many students also need direct spelling instruction. The second part of this chapter describes a workshop approach for teaching spelling. The third part of this chapter describes a variety of activities that may be used in the spelling workshop to help students develop as confident, capable spellers.

Spelling and the Writing Program

A third grader, frustrated by tedious spelling activities, wails to her mother, "Why do we have to learn to spell, anyway?" The answer is simple, yet profound: We have to learn to spell so we can write. For decades we tried to teach spelling for its own sake, without a comprehensive writing program to drive it. We "did spelling" every day, but only "did writing" when it fit into the schedule, when recess was rained out, or when we needed to fill some time quietly. We assigned topics, corrected and graded the results, and drove real, authentic writing underground. Then we were puzzled when children failed to learn either how to write powerfully or how to spell competently.

Today writing has taken its proper place in most classrooms, at the very center of language learning. Learning to write is as important as learning to read, and we now recognize that both aspects of literacy develop in concert with each other, each enhancing and encouraging the other. In recent years the process approach to writing instruction, pioneered by Donald Graves and Lucy McCormick Calkins, has revolutionized our teaching of language arts. The writing workshop, where students write from their own lives and assist each other in developing and refining their writing, has become the centerpiece of writing instruction.

Many teachers today are using a process writing approach, or writing workshop, in their classes. You may already be using a workshop approach to writing in your class. The following are the basic principles of process writing instruction.

1. *Give children ownership of their writing.* Ownership comes when children choose their own topics and write from their own experience. It comes when they retain control over their own pieces, choosing the form their writing will take and receiving help not only from the teacher but also from other writers. Ownership provides the impetus to craft and polish a piece, which includes editing and correcting spelling and other mechanical problems. Only when students retain ownership of a piece are they willing to invest the time and effort to craft and polish it. Thus, ownership is critical to students' ultimate desire to spell correctly.

2. *Teach writers how to use the writing cycle: prepare, write, revise, and edit.* Older methods of writing instruction focused on having students try to write both creatively and correctly at the same time. Rewriting was seen as the result of failed writing; only bad writing had to be rewritten. Utilizing the writing cycle teaches children to write in stages, with each stage having a separate focus. In early stages, the writer focuses on developing ideas, experimenting with forms and creating a message that can be read to others. In the middle of the writing cycle, the message is crafted; successive drafts help the writer clarify the message. Only in later stages, when what the writer wants to say is made clear, are mechanical

aspects such as spelling, grammar, and neatness emphasized. Emphasizing correct spelling should occur only after the writer has crafted the content to his or her satisfaction.

3. *Respond to the content before the form.* The purpose of writing is to convey a message. Responding to that message by commenting on what was written, asking the writer questions, or paraphrasing what was written helps the writer see that others can understand the writing. After you have responded to the message, it may be appropriate to respond to the form or mechanical aspects of the writing. But to respond first to form or appearance sends the wrong message to the writer: that the appearance of a piece is more important than its content. When writers receive this message, they begin to attend too much, or too soon, to superficial aspects of the writing. They may choose words they can spell correctly rather than words they really want to use. They may begin to write short, stilted pieces instead of writing authentically. They may concentrate on using their best handwriting rather than writing what they really want to say. All of these strategies short-circuit the writing process. Form *follows* the message; respond to the message first.

4. *Encourage collaboration.* Students learn at least as much, perhaps more, from each other as they do from their teachers. They also retain more control over their pieces when their peers make suggestions, for they often feel obliged to take teachers' suggestions. Too often students, especially younger ones, believe that teachers have all the answers. Thus, a teacher's casual suggestion may be heard as a requirement by young writers. They often feel freer to accept or reject the advice of peers. When struggling with spelling, students may also feel less embarrassment in asking for help from peers. Poor spellers in particular may feel shy about letting the teacher see how many errors they have made, but less so in getting help from classmates. Collaboration seems to help everyone.

5. *Provide correction judiciously and positively.* Some teachers cling to the notion that part of their job is to root out and correct every error, rather like zealous gardeners forever on guard against noxious weeds. But errors, in spelling or anything else, are not weeds

to be rooted out and burned. Errors are a natural by-product of learning; they are the result of taking risks, reaching out, and trying something new. Overly zealous correction teaches children to avoid risks and short-circuits the learning process. It teaches children to play it safe, which is the antithesis of good writing. Our job is not to correct every error, but to protect and nurture the self-esteem and confidence of every learner. We can do that best by correcting judiciously and selectively. Choose only a few errors to point out to the writer; limit what the writer is to do to make corrections. And remember to praise as well as correct; point out strengths as well as problems. Recognize the hard words that are spelled correctly, or the parts of a misspelled word that are correct. Respond to effort as well as achievement.

6. *Remember that each piece of writing is a risk a writer took.* Try to recall what it was like to turn in a piece of your own writing, or to share it with someone else. Few of us do so with unshakable confidence. We want our students to be more confident as writers than we were. We want them to be more willing to take risks, to stretch themselves, to share. That means that when we respond to writing we are responding to the *person* behind the writing. Respond to the writer as well as to the piece. Be gentle in correction and lavish with encouragement.

7. *Provide real outcomes for writing.* Turning in a piece of writing for teacher evaluation and a grade is not a real outcome, although it is the outcome most of us were limited to when we were learning to write. In traditional writing instruction, the teacher was usually the sole audience and judge of our writing. In a process-writing environment, real audiences are provided so that real writing may result. Work is continually shared in small and large groups. Stories are edited, bound, and published, and others read them. Letters are actually sent and replies expected. Written work is published, displayed, and shared. When writing has a real outcome, there is a real reason to edit and spell correctly. The impetus for correct spelling becomes the ability of others to read and understand it rather than to please the teacher or avoid having to write the paper again. Spelling in the classroom, then, assumes the same function it has in real life: to communicate clearly.

8. *Continue to learn how to improve your writing program.* Once you have your students writing actively, don't stop. Continue to read and learn about new approaches and strategies. The field of writing instruction is continually growing and changing. Share what you are reading and writing with others. (For a list of books on process writing and spelling, see the list provided at the end of this book.)

A Workshop Approach

One of the most exciting features of today's writing program is the workshop approach, described briefly in the preceding section. In addition, many teachers are now utilizing a workshop approach to reading, such as Nancie Atwell described in her book, *In the Middle* (1987). Atwell's workshop approach to teaching literature has been widely adapted by elementary teachers. These adaptations have led to many different ways of interpreting and implementing a workshop format, but several aspects are characteristic:

1. Students self-select much of what they will read.
2. Students work collaboratively with others, reading the same or related material, discussing and writing about what they are reading.
3. Students spend the majority of their instructional time reading and responding to the material in writing and other ways.
4. Skills and information students need are conveyed when needed in short, direct lessons to those students who need them.
5. Students keep track of their reading by self-monitoring and keeping personal records.
6. Students receive feedback from peers and teacher on their work in progress and their accomplishments.

The same characteristics that are the hallmarks of the workshop approach to writing and reading can be used to organize a workshop approach to spelling instruction. The fundamental aspects of this approach—self-selection, student ownership, self-monitoring, collaboration, group feedback, and needs-based direct instruction—can become the fundamentals of the spelling program as well.

Organizing for reading and writing instruction using a workshop format means that the teacher must accept a different role, that of an organizer, facilitator, and guide; it means organizing time, space, and materials differently than in a direct-instruction mode; and it means helping children establish ownership of their own work. In the same way, using a workshop approach for spelling instruction means organizing differently than in a direct-instruction or basal spelling approach. The basic tenets of the spelling workshop are establishing student ownership; organizing time, space, and materials; responding to students; and providing developmentally appropriate instruction when needed.

The role of the teacher

The spelling workshop teacher puts students' growth as spellers at the heart of the program. He or she recognizes that learning to spell is a developmental process that takes considerable time and effort to complete. The teacher recognizes, too, that students in the same grade, even at the same instructional reading level, differ widely in their present state of spelling development, and that these individual differences must drive the spelling curriculum. Thus, the teacher creates an environment in which individuals study words in a variety of ways that are appropriate to the student's present level of development and needs.

The teacher considers spelling an important part of literacy and plans for spelling study. What we consider important, we plan for systematically. We do not allow an important subject or process to just happen, or trust that development will occur without nurturing and attention. So the teacher creates a place in the curriculum and the schedule and a time for study that is systematic, predictable, and uninterrupted.

The spelling teacher helps children identify appropriate words and patterns for their study, using the language they use in speaking and writing and the language they read. He or she shows students how to identify misspelled words in their writing and extends their understanding by relating words to common patterns, related words, and derivations. He or she provides a variety of strategies and activities by which students can learn correct spellings and extend their word knowledge, and encourages students to choose activities they find most helpful and compelling. He or she provides a variety of ways for students to monitor, evaluate, and celebrate their progress.

And he or she helps students set reasonable goals for the number and type of new words that will be learned.

Organizing time

Even in a print-rich environment, spelling development does not just happen for many children. There must be a predictable period of time set aside each day for the specific, intentional study of words and their spellings. A period of about fifteen minutes a day, or seventy-five minutes a week, is desirable. During that time, students engage in a variety of activities that focus on the spelling, meaning, and use of selected words in speaking and writing. This is not simply an extension of the writing workshop, but a time set aside for intensive study of words and spelling patterns. A basic plan for such time might look like this:

- *Monday:* Students develop their list of words for the week's study with assistance from the teacher, identifying words from their writing folders and other words they wish to learn. Individual weekly lists are compiled. Depending on their age, developmental level, and other factors, students may contract with the teacher to aim for a particular number of new or troublesome words. For younger students and/or less able spellers, aiming for four or five new words per week is probably sufficient, while older or more proficient spellers may aim for eight, ten, or even more.

- *Tuesday, Wednesday, and Thursday:* Workshop activities are undertaken in groups, pairs, and individually. (A variety of developmentally appropriate activities for workshop use are described in the latter part of this chapter.) Workshop activities may include spelling games, group work on common patterns, word building, activities to strengthen visual memory, work with word families, rhyming, dictionary activities, and proofreading. Thursday may also be used as a pretest or practice-test day.

- *Friday:* Students are tested on the words they selected for study that week, and progress is celebrated. Student partners may be used to test each other, with one reading the words while the other writes them; responsible students may also check each other's work. Students record "New Words I Can Spell" in their personal spelling logs. Words that students choose to continue working on may be carried over to the next week's list.

Establishing student ownership

A fundamental aspect of any workshop approach is that students maintain ownership of their work. Ownership is established in the spelling workshop by encouraging students to use their writing as a basis for selecting words to study. Troublesome high-frequency words, words from current reading and content subjects, and other interesting words may be added by mutual agreement. Developmentally appropriate word lists featuring words sharing a common pattern may be available as another source of words for selection, as described in Chapter 7. Certainly the teacher may select some of the words to be studied, but the major emphasis should be on the students' self-selection of words they need to learn to spell. Student ownership is maintained by the students' own record keeping, including spelling logs and lists of mastered words.

Responding to students' work

Spellers need feedback on their efforts and progress. As we said earlier, teacher correction should be undertaken judiciously and with a positive tone. Emphasis should be placed on helping students identify those words in their writing that they are uncertain about, rather than on the teacher's marking every misspelling. Students should be encouraged to work together in identifying and studying words, since typically more than one student will need to work on the same or similar words or patterns.

Positive feedback is critically important in developing positive attitudes about spelling. For this reason, teachers should remember to systematically call students' attention to words and patterns spelled correctly, "logical" errors, and previously misspelled words now used correctly. Progress should not be measured solely by test results, but even more importantly by the correct use of words studied previously. Bulletin boards, positive notes home, praise, and other means should be used to make sure that all students are rewarded and encouraged, not just the best spellers or those mastering the most new words at one time. Depending on the age of students, rewards for progress and sustained effort for individuals, groups, or the whole class may be made. Such rewards may include stickers, buttons, a special snack, extra free reading or game time, "Star Speller" ribbons, an art activity, lunch outside or with the teacher, names on a special poster, or the opportunity to take a special stuffed animal, trophy, game, puzzle, or plaque home for the night or weekend. Rewards in which everyone can participate are particularly effective, as they de-emphasize competition and encourage cooperative learning and group spirit.

Spelling Workshop Activities

In the rest of this chapter, we describe a variety of strategies that may be used in the spelling workshop to help children become automatic, independent spellers. The various activities have different levels of difficulty and allow children of different spelling abilities to benefit from them. They are designed to minimize teaching time but maximize student thinking time. Most important, they are *real;* that is, they develop and reinforce spelling skills within the context of reading, writing, and studying words by comparing, contrasting, and associating them. Students are actively engaged in doing something, rather than watching or filling in blanks.

Activities for Precommunicative and Semiphonetic Spellers

As you may recall from chapter 3, precommunicative spellers have not yet discovered the alphabetic principle, that letters stand for sounds in words we say. Their writing is intended to communicate but not to represent speech sounds. It is made up of random letters and letterlike signs. Semiphonetic spellers have made the alphabetic discovery, and they attempt to represent some sounds in their writing, but their spelling attempts are incomplete and may be difficult to read. Both these spelling stages often correspond to the prereading and just-beginning-to-read stages, and are typical of older preschoolers, kindergartners, and many first graders. Activities for these young spellers must meet their special needs in order to foster their growth as writers and spellers.

They need to practice phonemic segmentation, the ability to mentally hold onto and manipulate sounds and syllables in words, which is the basic process in "sounding out." They need to develop the concept of word, the understanding that written words have beginnings and ends and are bounded by spaces, although spoken words may not have noticeable boundaries and may seem to run together in a stream.

Spellers at these stages need to practice letter-sound correspondence; that is, they should attempt to represent the sounds in the words they say with letters as they try to write them. They need to practice saying words and listening to the sounds in them, particularly the beginning consonant sounds at first, and matching those sounds to consonant letters they know.

Perhaps most important, they need to write often, every day, about things that are real and important to them, with the emphasis and attention placed on the message, not on the form it takes or the correctness of the language or spelling. They need to see themselves as writers, full of wonderful ideas and competent to put those ideas down in pictures, in scribbles, in pretend writing, and in writing they and others can read (with help, usually). They need to practice putting down the words they want to use on paper without limiting their word choices to the words they can spell. They need to invent spellings for words they do not know, so that they put their messages first and continually practice matching sounds to letters. The activities that follow will help precommunicative and semiphonetic spellers to practice and develop these important abilities.

To develop letter-sound correspondence

The following activities are designed to develop letter-sound correspondence.

Beginning sound brainstorming. For any consonant letter being studied, write the letter on the board and brainstorm with children words that begin with the letter's most common sound; give a few examples to start them off. Print the words on the board as they are offered, and have children come forward and underline the beginning letter as all repeat the word. Emphasize the beginning sound when saying the word.

Picture sorts. Sort picture cards into groups that share the same initial sound. Commercial sets of picture cards are widely available from school supply catalogs and teaching supply stores, and may also be available at better toy stores. Preselect pictures of objects beginning with two or more selected sounds and shuffle them together; distribute cards among the group. Show an example card for each sound, repeat the word, and place the example cards at the top of the pocket chart or tape them to the board. Have children come forward with their cards individually to name the picture on their cards and place their cards under the correct example card.

Stand-up sorts. Instead of placing their cards in the correct category, have each child hold his or her card so everyone can see it and stand in the correct group next to or behind the child holding the example card.

Oral matching. Say a word with a selected beginning sound and invite children to match its beginning sound with a word of their own. Then switch roles: a child names a word and you say another one; the child says whether they match at the beginning or not.

Auditory discrimination. Give each child some means of physically indicating "same" and "different": an individual reversible sign, two file cards with "same" and "different" printed on them, a red card for "same" and a blue card for "different," or whatever. Then pronounce word pairs or threes and have each one in the group hold up the correct card or sign simultaneously if the words have the same beginning (or ending) sound, or different sounds. (Watch for children who have to look at someone else's card before they can hold up their own: either they don't understand the task, or they are having trouble distinguishing between the sounds. Either way, they need extra help.)

To develop phonemic segmentation

The following activities may help develop phonemic segmentation.

Syllable clap. Teach children how to clap once for each syllable in spoken words, and then practice a little every day; say a word in a natural way, and then repeat it with each syllable emphasized as the children chant it and clap once for each syllable. For example: "Chicken; chick-en" (with two claps); "butterfly; but-ter-fly" (with three claps). Let individuals take the teacher's role as soon as they are ready to.

Sound clap. When syllables are well mastered, move to awareness of individual speech sounds in words, and follow the same procedure as above but have children clap for each phoneme. How many sounds do you hear in, for example, *cat?* There are three sounds: /k/ /ă/ /t/. Pronounce the word normally, then separate each sound with a brief space and clap for each sound. Keep the words short, as it is too difficult for young children to break down long words into their component sounds; it overloads short-term memory.

Sound counters. This is a version of Sound Clapping, except that instead of clapping, children place counters (dried beans, Bingo chips, buttons, whatever) in a row to correspond with the number of phonemes.

To develop concept of word

The following activities are designed to develop children's concept of word.

Big book sharing. One of the best ways to develop and reinforce the concept of word is choral reading (often called shared reading) of Big Books and stories dictated and written on chart tablets. The teacher points to each written word as it is read. These stories should be read and reread until they can be recited fluently. Children should practice reciting and pointing to each word as it is read.

Voice pointing. With individual copies of dictated stories, trade book editions of Big Books, and memorized trade books, children should practice reciting and pointing to each word as it is read. Emphasis should be placed on rapid pointing and on reading/reciting at a normal talking speed, not in a slow, word-by-word fashion. Children should practice quickly finding and pointing to individual words throughout the story as they are called out by the teacher or a partner.

Stand-up sentences. Print the first sentence from a familiar Big Book, dictated story, poem, or song on a long strip of tagboard. Leave slightly larger-than-usual spaces between the words. Choral-read the sentence. While the children watch, cut between each word with scissors and hand each individual word to a child. (You may cut between the last word and the period, and give one child the period.)

Have the children get up and stand in the right order, left to right, to make the sentence by holding their cards in front of them. (You may explain that the period is necessary to show where the sentence ends.) Then have the sentence read either by the "words" themselves, with each child saying his or her own word in order, or by the rest of the group as you point to or stand behind each "word." Continue in this way through the rest of the book or story, making sure each child in the group gets to "be a word" at least once. When the group is finished, put all the word cards in a zip-locking plastic bag and store with the book or story.

Words on the floor.   Put the Big Book or copy of the dictated story from the Stand-up Sentences activity above in the center. Have one child or a pair read the text again and lay out all the word cards on the floor in the correct order. Make sure they mix up the cards before putting them back in the plastic bag for the next time.

Hide-a-word.   Place the word cards that make up one of the sentences in their correct order in a pocket chart. After choral-reading the sentence, tell all the children to cover their eyes tightly. Then, turn over one of the word cards to hide it. At your signal, all the children uncover their eyes and try to figure out which word was hidden. Choose a child to be the "word hider" next time, and have him or her choose the next player. If one sentence is too easy, use two or even three sentences in order from the original text.

Add-a-word.   Distribute a number of word cards among the group, making sure that nouns, simple verbs, prepositions, and describing words like color words and numbers are included. Have two children stand up, with their word cards creating a short sentence or phrase like "dogs walk" or "one car." One at a time, have words added that increase the length of the sentence while still making sense, such as "dogs go for a walk" or "one small green car under a tree." Kids like silly sentences even more than "sensible" ones; "green dogs go for a drive" or "one small green car in the sky" can be even better! Make sure everyone gets to be a word several times.

To develop willingness to invent spellings while writing

The following activities encourage invented spelling.

Demonstrate invention.   On a transparency, chart tablet, or the board, show beginning writers the many ways there are to write a message. First, draw a picture; don't try to make it perfect, for children will be more likely to risk drawing even if they think they aren't very good at it if you are willing to take the risk first! Talk about your picture. Then, write a sentence or two about it using invented spelling, sounding out the words aloud as you do so. Explain that many children invent the spellings of words they aren't sure of in this way. Then, write the sentences in standard spelling, explaining that this is the way adults would spell those words, as they would see them in books. Finally, show how a writer could write as much of the word as she or he could and draw a line for the rest of the word. Encourage children to use invented spellings and to spell as much of the words as they can when they write.

Group invention.   If a group is going to write on a common topic, say Halloween, brainstorm with the group words they want to use. When a child suggests a word, invite each one to try to write the word on a piece of scratch paper. Then call on several to spell out their invented versions, and list these on the board. Make encouraging remarks about these inventions as you list them. Point out that all inventions are approximations, that they are useful when writers are trying to get their ideas down on paper, and that help will be available when it is time to make a final draft. Finally, write the correct spelling at the top of each column of inventions.

Activities for Semiphonetic and Phonetic Spellers

Semiphonetic and phonetic spellers depend largely on the sounds they hear in words as they spell. They also depend on these letter-sound relationships as they read unfamiliar words. Word recognition skills and spelling concepts develop together and can reinforce each other for beginning readers and writers. The following activities will help your students solidify their understanding of letter-sound relationships in reading and writing.

To develop letter-sound relationships
Here are some activities for letter-sound relationships.

Word hunts. These may be done orally without reference to the written form of the words, thus focusing children's attention on the sound feature; or they may be done in combination with the written form of the words, by listing words on the board as they are offered. Either way, start by providing two or three examples of words that have a common beginning sound; say, *ball, bears,* and *butter* for the /b/ sound. Have children look all around the room and offer other words that begin with the same sound. If you are focusing only on the sound, repeat the words as they are offered. If you are pairing the words and their written forms, write the words under the example words as they are offered. In the latter case, remember that some sounds have more than one spelling; *cat* and *kittens* start with the same sound but different letters, as do *fox* and *phone.* If children provide such examples, simply point out that some sounds have more than one spelling and focus on the way these letter combinations sound.

Picture sorts. As described in the previous section, distribute picture cards among the children and set up one or two pictures as examples of each beginning sound, then have children come up and place their cards with the appropriate example, saying the word as they do so. The example cards may be placed in a pocket chart with the picture cards in an envelope and put in a center for individual sorting also.

Stand-up sorts. As before, give one child an example card and have all those with pictures of things with the same beginning sound come up and form a group or line next to the example card. Repeat for each beginning sound being studied.

Cut, paste, and label. Create a large poster headed with one or more pictures of things with the same beginning sound. Distribute magazines or catalogs, scissors, and paste. Have children find pictures of things with the same beginning sound, cut them out, and paste them on the poster. As a group, name each thing and label it. Display the poster and review the words on it as you review the sound.

Draw and label. This may be done on one large poster or on individual sheets of paper. Younger children may fold a sheet of

71

paper horizontally and vertically to create four large spaces. Brainstorm, then have the children draw an object beginning with the target sound and label each picture. Display the work.

Picture and word sort.   When children are facile with picture sorting, use picture cards and separate cards with the printed word for each picture. Sort the picture cards by beginning sound, then have the children with word cards attempt to match the word cards with the corresponding pictures.

Name sorts.   Print each child's first name on a tagboard strip or large card and distribute them. Print each alphabet letter above the chalk tray in order. Beginning with *A,* have all children whose names begin with that letter come up and place their name cards under the letter. Discuss which letters have more than one name, which ones have none, and which letters are the most common. For each letter that begins a name, brainstorm with children other words or other names that begin with the same sound/letter. Name cards may also be sorted by the number of letters in each first name, the number of syllables in each name, and the like.

Magazine search.   Magazines and newspapers are good sources of words, phrases, and sentences with a particular feature, such as same beginning sounds, initial consonants, blends, and endings. Specify the feature to be found, such as "words that start like *ball* and *back*" or "words that end like *washed* and *started*" and have students cut out examples, pasting them on a poster or individual sheets. Review the words they find and have them underline or circle the featured part. Display the work.

To teach word families and rhyming words
The following activities encourage the learning of word families and rhyming words.

Teaching rhyming.   Some younger children may need practice in the concept of rhyming before they can benefit from the activities that follow. Teach rhyming orally at first, by giving an example word and then creating sentences that end in a word that rhymes. For example, if the key word is *head,* sentences might be "I made a sandwich with peanut butter and . . . [bread]" or "Good night, it's time to go to. . . . [bed]" Make up lots of such examples, doing one pattern every day, until everyone is facile with the operation of rhyming.

Name rhymes.   Choose a student's name card that can be rhymed with other words, such as *Jenny*. Say pairs of words, only some of which rhyme, like *Jenny/penny* and *Jenny/little*. When the pairs rhyme, the children can point at Jenny and call out her name. When the pairs don't rhyme, they should shake their heads silently.

Rhyming word sorts.   Distribute picture cards or word cards of words that rhyme. Provide a picture card or word card as an example of the pattern. Have children place their cards under the example of the pattern that fits and say all the words in the category. This can also be done as a Stand-up Sort by having the children stand in groups holding their word or picture cards in front of them.

Word families.   Word families are groups of rhyming words made by changing the first letter or letter group; for example, *bat-sat-cat-rat-fat-hat-pat,* or *keep-sleep-creep-deep-weep.* For any word family, write as many words with the same pattern as you can think of on tagboard strips, then carefully cut between the beginning letter(s) and the word stem (*-at, -eep*). Put the word stems in a column on a pocket chart; distribute the initial letters among the children. Model making the words by placing one letter to the left of the stem to make a whole word (*deep,* for example). Then have children come to the pocket chart and place their letters to the left of a stem to create a new word; as each word is made, have the whole group say it. Write all the words in one family on a large chart and display it.

More word families.   On a duplicating master, make a list of words in a word family, lining up the beginning sounds and the stems under each other. Duplicate and distribute. Have each child cut out the words and cut between the beginning sounds and the stems, as above. Have them lay out the stems in a column on their desks. As you call out a word, have them place the correct letter or letter pair to the left of the stem to create the word. When finished they should have a column of completed words on their desks. These may be glued onto paper and illustrated, creating individual word family charts.

"Guess My Rhyme" game.   Using word family and rhyme charts or other charts as sources, have children find words that fit certain clues—for example, "This word starts like *happy* and rhymes with *Bill*" (*hill*). Repeat using other patterns.

Rhyming books.   Read and share lots of rhyming books and poems in class. Books like *One Fish, Two Fish, Red Fish, Blue Fish; Hop on Pop; The Day the Goose Got Loose;* and *Let's Marry, Said the Cherry* are always popular with children and give them good experience hearing and manipulating rhymes and word families. (Many Big Books are rhyming books.)

"Hinky Pinkies".   "Hinky Pinkies" are rhyming riddles with two-syllable words. "Hink Pinks" are rhyming pairs with one syllable each. Children love to try to solve the riddles and make up their own. Here are some examples of "Hink Pinks":

- What do you call a swimming dog? A *wet pet.*
- What do you call a man in a boa contrictor costume? A *fake snake.*
- What do you call a chicken coop? A *hen pen.*

Here are some examples of "Hinky Pinkies":

- What do you call a rabbit that tells jokes? A *funny bunny.*
- What do you call a dog that fell in the river? A *soggy doggie.*

Illustrated "Hink Pinks".   Brainstorm with your students as many rhyming pairs as they can come up with, list them, and have students illustrate their favorites. These can be bound into class books. (Bruce Macmillan's *One Sun* is a whole book of two-word "terse verse" using this pattern.)

To develop visual memory and the visual coding mechanism

Good spellers seem to be able to tell when a misspelled word doesn't look right, and they seem to be able to mentally see a word when they try to spell it. Both of these abilities are based on visual memory and visual coding. Although people probably differ in terms of how good they are at visual memory, we believe that all children can be taught to develop these abilities to some extent and to sharpen their visual memory skills. These abilities have important implications for their spelling and word recognition abilities. The following activities are arranged roughly in order from simplest to most challenging.

Remembering pictures.   Have children study a picture for a specified length of time, say for thirty seconds. Then remove the picture and have them recall and describe as much detail as they can from the picture. Put the picture back and have them point out the things they recalled and some elements that were forgotten.

Kim's Game.   This is the classic objects-on-the-tray game that Rudyard Kipling described in *Kim*. Place a variety of small objects on a table, desk, or tray and cover them with a cloth. Students may work in small groups of three or four or as a whole class. When you uncover the collection, each student is to try to memorize as many objects as possible and remember them. Uncover the tray for a period of seconds, then cover it again. Have each group list as many objects as they can remember. Recheck to see what was recalled and what was forgotten. Work toward adding to the number of objects gradually.

Kim's Game II.   As students get better at Kim's Game and can recall almost all of the objects, make the game a little more complex. After they have studied the array, remove one object under the cloth so they can't see it. The object now is to determine what's missing. This can be made even more challenging by both removing one object and rearranging the rest.

Memory sentences.   Write a sentence on the board with words that most or all of the students can spell easily. Some teachers use day-and-date sentences, positive statements like "I'll try my best today," or quotations. Choral-read the sentence and have students look carefully at each word. Then cover the sentence with a tagboard strip and have students try to write the sentence from memory. Uncover the sentence and have them note to themselves words they missed or misspelled. Don't make a test out of this; its purpose is to have children do a bit of visual memory practice every day. Kids will gradually get better at it.

Sorting words by length. Use the word cards from the Big Book activities, children's word bank cards, or word cards of the spelling words being studied. Pass them out to the children. Write each numeral, 1 through 10 or so, on sheets of paper. Hold up the 1 and have all the children holding cards with one-letter words come up and show their word cards. Have the group read and spell each word and put the cards on the chalk ledge in front of the numeral. Continue with two-letter words, then three-letter words, and so forth. Word cards and numerals may be placed in a center for individual practice.

Making words. For this activity, students need letter holders and letter cards. Letter holders may be made by cutting a file folder in half on the fold, folding the bottom an inch up, and stapling at intervals to form four or five pockets. Letter cards are made by cutting file cards into one-by-two-inch rectangles. Write a lowercase letter on the top of each card, leaving the lower inch blank to insert into the holder; write the uppercase counterpart on the reverse. Consonants and vowels may be written in two different colors. There should be a complete set of letters for each child and two or three times as many of the most common letters. Letters may be stored in zip-closing plastic bags or labeled storage boxes for convenience in passing them out and collecting them. Pass out the letters needed to make words in a particular word family; for example, *a* and *b, d, g, h, l, m, p, r, s, t,* and *y.* Have children place their vowel letter and *y* in the middle of their holders. Demonstrate with large letter cards in your pocket chart or on the chalk ledge. Then as you call out words and give a context sentence, have children put the consonant letters in their holders to make these words: *bay, day, gay, hay, lay, may, pay, ray, say, stay, play,* and *tray.* As each word is made, have a child come up and make the word in your pocket chart or on the board with the large letter cards. Have them say each word and chant the letters, and correct any mistakes in their own letter holders. Repeat with other word family patterns.

More making words. Distribute a variety of consonants and vowels, and call out words that require the children to change initial and final letters and vowels too, such as *pat, bag, hot, tap, top, not, bat,* and so forth. As before, display each word with the large letter cards so all can see it and have the children chant the letters.

Making words with tactile letters. Students enjoy the novelty of working with letters that have textural interest. Have children make their spelling words or word families with letters cut from sandpaper, textured wallpaper, or felt or with commercial linking letters, plastic or magnetic letters, or foam puzzle letters. (Cutting the letters from sandpaper and other textured papers is a job parent volunteers can do at home.)

Chanting letters. As children write spelling words, have them chant the letters aloud. This is an aid to remembering words, as it links the letter names and their order with the visual representation of the words. They should practice writing the words as quickly as they can while chanting the letters. Neatness does not count in this activity!

Finger-tracing. Have children trace letters on word cards with a finger as they chant the letters. This activity helps to link letter names, order, the visual representation, and the tactile shape of the letters all at once. Many children need to let the hand help the memory in this way.

Progressive exposure. This activity, first suggested by Don Holdaway in *The Foundations of Literacy* (1979), features the reading of predictable text with some words or phrases hidden by cardboard strips. Holdaway used text on a transparency, which works very well, but Big Books are perfect. Cover part of a line by paper-clipping a tagboard strip to the edge of the page; cover individual words with file cards held in place with doubled-sided tape or memo papers with a sticky strip on the reverse. As you choral-read the story and come to a covered word or phrase, encourage students to use context to predict what will come next; then uncover the first word of the phrase, or first letter of the word, and confirm or change the predictions. Uncover the word or phrase, read it, and go on. This is a good way to highlight spelling patterns you are studying as they occur in meaningful text. Note the word and its pattern, then go on with the reading.

Homographs. Homographs are words that are spelled the same way but have different meanings and may have different pronunciations; for example, *bow* (noun) and *bow* (verb), *lead* (noun) and *lead* (verb), *read* (present tense) and *read* (past tense) are all homographs. Work with these in sentence contexts; put sentence strips on the board with a blank space for the spelling word, and distribute homograph word cards. As each sentence is read, have a child come up and place the homograph card in the sentence.

Homophones. Homophones have the same pronunciation, but different meanings and perhaps different spellings, such as *wood* and *would, plane* and *plain, read* and *reed*. As above, use sentence strips and have students place the correct word in the sentence to complete the meaning.

What looks right? Identify a rhyming pattern that has two different spellings; for example, *-ane* and *-ain, -ite* and *-ight, -eek* and *-eak*. Write an example of each pattern at the top of two columns on the board. Give two students dictionaries and the job of being spelling checkers; all others have paper and pencils. Say a word that fits one of the two spelling patterns and give a context sentence; write it both ways on the board, once under each example word; for example, in the sentence "The sun is very ——— today," is the spelling word *brite* or *bright?* (One spelling must be incorrect, of course.) Have students predict which spelling "looks right" and write the word under the correct example word, while the checkers check their dictionaries for the correct spelling. Erase the incorrect spelling and have students make any necessary corrections on their papers. This activity helps students see that rhyming is an important clue to the spelling of similar words, but that seeing if it "looks right" is also important.

Look-cover-write-check. This is an efficient study method that maximizes the visual coding mechanism. Students should *never* copy spelling words, but rather should look carefully at the correct spelling, then cover it and attempt to write it from memory. Mere copying does not help children remember words; writing from memory helps to sharpen visual memory and make children more independent.

Word wall. Pat Cunningham suggests (in *Phonics They Use,* 1991) a number of uses for posters or bulletin boards containing commonly used words often misspelled, special content-area vocabulary, and similar collections of words. These may have picture or sentence clues or be placed in alphabetical order or some other category system (math words, weather words, color words, and so forth). The posters or bulletin boards serve as visual reminders when children are writing or proofreading. However, it is important to remind them that they should never copy words from the wall; copying will not help them become better spellers. Instead the words are there as reminders; they should find and look carefully at the word, then try to write it from memory and check it on the wall.

Find a word. Once a day, call out a commonly used word or commonly misspelled word you want your students to review. Give them a chance to find it, then point to it yourself; have students chant the letters, then write it from memory as you cover the word with your hand, a piece of paper, or whatever. Then uncover the word and have students check their work. Each day, have them find, chant, and write one or more words for quick review.

Rhyme review. Like previously described rhyming activities, this one features commonly misspelled words from the Word Wall. Give a rhyme and meaning clue—for example, "This word rhymes with *yes* and it goes in this sentence: 'If you are not sure, take a ———— ' "; or "This word rhymes with *creature* and it means someone who teaches children." Children should write the words from memory as you give the clues; afterward review the answers, point to the words on the wall, and have the children chant the spelling and correct their mistakes.

Making words again. In this activity, children make words from the Word Wall with letter cards, letter cubes, linking letters, and the like. Students in second grade and beyond can easily make their own letter cards or letter cubes by printing two or three copies of each letter (six or more of the common consonants and vowels) in lined squares on a duplicated sheet and then cutting on the lines. Then, as words are called out, they locate the necessary letters and place them in order on their desks. They then check their spellings with those on the wall and make changes as needed.

Read my mind. Have students number a piece of scrap paper from one to five. As you call out a clue, have them write a word from the wall they think is the answer next to each number, spelling it from memory. Clue number one is that the word is from the Word Wall. Clues two through five help the students narrow the possibilities; for example, clue two may be "It starts with a T"; three might be "It has three syllables"; four might be "It is a time-related word" and five might be "It rhymes with *borrow*." By the time you get to five, the children will already have figured out that the word is *tomorrow*.

Making big words. This is another activity using the letter cards or letter squares. Younger students may want to use their letter holders. Write on the board a long, polysyllabic word from a content-area lesson or story being read. Have children select letter cards for all the letters in that word. In a given amount of time, have them make as many two-letter words as they can, then as many three-letter words, and so forth. Write all the two-letter words they make on the board; repeat for the three-letter words, the four-letter words, and so forth. Finally, erase the long word from the board and have them make the long word from memory with their letters. Demonstrate the use of the dictionary to check any spellings the students are unsure of, or to check if any unusual words are really words!

Wheel of Fortune. The popular TV game show "Wheel of Fortune" can be adapted as a spelling game. Write the category of a word on the board (an occupation, a weather word, a history word, whatever) and draw a line for each letter in the word. Have one student guess "Is there a(n) ——?", naming a letter, vowel or consonant. If the letter is in the word, fill it in where it belongs and give the student a paper clip or some other counter. That student continues until he or she guesses a letter that is not in the word; then it becomes someone else's turn. The entire word must be spelled out before the word can be "guessed." The person who correctly fills in the final letters gets a bonus of five counters. The player (or team) with the most counters at the end of the game wins.

80

Activities for Transitional and Conventional Spellers

In about grade three and beyond, students begin to be aware of more than just the sound and visual memory of words they want to spell. They begin to attend to word parts such as prefixes (parts added to the beginning of a base word), suffixes (parts added to the ends of words), base or root words, and syllables. Facility with these word parts can speed spelling development in the middle grades and beyond.

To develop awareness of structural patterns

Here are some activities to develop awareness of structural patterns.

Prefix of the week.   Select one of the prefixes from the chart in Appendix A each week. Have students look up the prefix in several different dictionaries and compare the etymology (word history) given in each dictionary. Brainstorm and list as many words as can be thought of that begin with the prefix; then search comprehensive dictionaries for others students may have forgotten. Have them try to explain what the prefix means in each word. These words, written on posters, may become part of the Word Wall.

Word search race.   List words beginning with a certain prefix, as above. Have students work in teams to search newspapers and magazines for as many occurrences of those words, or others with the same prefix, as they can find in a given amount of time. Words found may be cut out and glued to a sheet of paper, circled, or highlighted; at the end of the time period each team counts all the words it found and checks to make sure that each one found really belongs to that category; for example, for the prefix *re-*, *replay*, *repossess*, and *recant* would be acceptable, but *really* and *readership* would not. The team with the most acceptable words at the end wins.

Latin lives.   Each week choose one of the Latin stems listed in Appendix A. As with the prefix activity above, have the stem checked in several different dictionaries. Then brainstorm words from this base, and look them up in dictionaries to check their derivation. An etymological dictionary such as Skeat's *Concise Etymological Dictionary of the English Language* can be of great help. Do the Word Search Race as above with words sharing the same base or derivation.

Big word of the day. Each day let a student select one "big word" from a story currently being read, a newspaper article, or a content subject area to be the Big Word of the Day for the next day. The next day, write a sentence on the board containing the big word that helps to suggest its meaning. Take the word apart, looking for its base word, its affixes, and their meanings, and listing other words it is related to. Then recheck the word's meaning by having a student read the sentence and explain the word's meaning. After you have done this a number of times, students will begin to take the word apart and look for its related forms almost automatically.

Compound words. List on the board three or four compound words from a particular story or content lesson. For each example, think of an many other words as possible that have the same base word; for example, *snowflake, snowstorm, snowbank, snowsuit, snowman,* and so forth. Younger students may want to list and illustrate these as a compound word family.

Crazy compounds. List several categories of compound words, then have students create original compound words by combining the word parts in new ways, such as *starbird, rainflower,* or *rattleworm.* What would such new things look like? Have them illustrate and share their inventions.

Concentration. This game may be played as a group with large cards, or in a center with smaller cards. Two players or teams compete. First, make a set of word cards; half of the cards have a common prefix or suffix written on them, such as *re-, non-, -er, -ment,* and the like; the other cards have base words that can be combined with the affixes to create real words you want your students to be able to spell, such as *rebuild, nonstop, teacher,* or *entertainment.* Of course, not all stems will combine with all the affixes to make real words. Shuffle the cards together and lay them face down in horizontal and vertical rows; the more cards, the more challenging the game is. Teams or players take turns turning over a specified number of cards, like four or six at a time; if any two cards turned over can be combined into a real word, the team removes and keeps those two cards. The team with the most pairs at the end wins. Another way to play is to leave all cards in the array, but award two points for each pair located. At the end of a turn all the cards are turned back over but left in their same location, and the other team takes a turn.

Wheel of Fortune. As described in the previous section, this version of the popular TV game is played by two teams. Players take turns guessing letters in a mystery word, filling in letters as they correctly guess them until they are able to identify the word.

Read my mind. In this activity you choose a word with an affix being studied—for example, *nonstop*. As described previously, students number scrap paper from one to five and attempt to guess the mystery word in less than five attempts as you give increasingly specific clues. In our example, the first clue might be "It is a member of the *non-* family." Succeeding clues might be "It has seven letters," "It is associated with airplanes," "It has two syllables," and "It rhymes with *drop*."

What looks right? This activity combines visual memory with structural analysis, as you try to help students distinguish between similar-sounding affixes such as *-able* and *ible, -tion* and *-sion, -aly* and *-ily,* and the like. Two students are assigned to be dictionary checkers; the others choose, or vote on, which form of a word looks right. One version of the word uses the correctly spelled affix, while the other uses an incorrect affix (for example, *dependable* and *dependible*).

To develop awareness of derivational patterns

Spellers at the transitional stage who are in the middle grades and beyond need to develop a level of spelling awareness that goes beyond the sounds in words to a deeper level of relationships between and among words. These semantic, or meaning, patterns are encoded in base words and affixes, described above, and in the related or derived forms of words sharing the same base. For example, *receive, receiver, received, receiving, receipt, receivership, reception, receptionist,* and *receptor* are derived forms of the same word, and *receiving line, receiving blanket,* and *receiving end* are related phrases or expressions. Study of the relations between such groups of words gives transitional spellers a means of mastering many new words.

Concentration. Like the activity described above, in Concentration two players or teams attempt to find as many related pairs as possible. Make a word card set that contains many pairs of related words (for example, various related forms of *receive, decide, remember,* and *motion* could be used), write them on cards, shuffle them, and lay them out in horizontal and vertical rows. Players take turns turning over pairs of cards. If they are related forms of the same word, they keep the pair and get points; if they are not related, the cards are turned back over and the other player or team tries. It helps to remember where cards are in the array as they are turned over!

What looks right?, Read my mind, **and** ***Wheel of Fortune.*** These are all good activities to reinforce the relationships between derived forms, just as they are for structural patterns. Play as described previously.

Word hunt race. This game may be played in groups or teams. Give a Latin or Greek stem from the lists in Appendix A or a common base word such as *move.* In a given time period, teams are to brainstorm as many related forms of the word as they can think of and list them. Lists are checked for correctness, and the team with the most related forms wins that round.

Word sorts. Word sorts are as useful for students dealing with derived forms as for younger students dealing with letter-sound relationships and other spelling features. Done in groups or individually, they require students to sort word cards into categories sharing a common feature. For example, groups of words with prefixes such as *non-, sub-, re-,* or *inter-,* with endings such as *-tion, -able, -ly* or *-ment* or with the base word in common such as *remove, motion, commotion, demote,* and *promoted* could be placed in a deck. Students form their own categories, explaining the common feature shared by all the words in a group. When word lists are used in which a number of the words fit a particular category, individual word sorts can be done by writing the words in columns on a duplicated sheet and having students cut the words apart and sort the pieces on their desks.

Derivation race. Working in teams, students race to locate as many different derived forms of the same word as possible in a given amount of time from magazines and newspapers. These may be circled, underlined, or highlighted or they may be cut out and glued in columns to sheets of paper. (The latter takes more time, but it makes students sort the words as they go.) Alternatively, they may search for as many instances of words with a particular feature, such as a Greek or Latin prefix or ending. The group with the most words that correctly fit the category, without duplications, wins.

Charades. A version of the familiar game of Charades, here students draw a card with either a derived form of a base word or a common Greek or Latin prefix on it, and have to act it out silently. Instead of guessing aloud, students have to either write on the board the word they think is being acted out or hold up a card with the word written on it. This game may be played with individuals acting and guessing, or with three teams: one acting and two competing to guess the answer first. Have the teams take turns being the actors.

Summary

In this chapter we have described the critical role of writing in learning to spell, and we outlined the main principles of the writing workshop and reading workshop approach. We described how the workshop approach may be applied to spelling instruction. We described a wide variety of activities to use in the spelling workshop with spellers at different developmental levels. Memorizing and copying are replaced by more enjoyable activities that have students make letter-sound correspondences, use context and word meanings, and categorize words based on shared features. The activities are grouped according to the spelling and word knowledge skills generally developed by students at a particular spelling stage.

7

Choosing Spelling Words

EVERY TEACHER NEEDS to know how to select words that are appropriate for his or her students to study. Many teachers make up their own weekly spelling lists. Others use word lists provided by spelling basals, often adapting these lists to their own needs by adding words students frequently misspell in their writing and words from content subjects and books students are reading, or by shortening the lists. This chapter will help you learn how to choose words for your students to study, whether you make up your own lists or adapt commercial ones.

When considering basal spelling lists, teachers often wonder how the words are selected. Almost all publishers of commercial spelling programs use the same base of research as their foundation. This research consists of word usage studies. Researchers collect thousands of writing samples of students at various grade levels and determine which words students actually use in their writing. This is useful because we know that people generally use only a fraction of the words in English in their writing. You can probably think of many examples of words you and your students can read and understand easily, but almost never use in writing. On the other hand, we use many of the same words over and over; about 5,000 words account for over 90 percent of the words used in writing. The thinking behind the usage studies is that by determining which words students use often and then teaching everyone to spell those words, writing would be made easier and more enjoyable.

Word frequency refers to how often a word occurs in written English. You can probably think of a dozen or more frequently occurring words in only a few seconds: *and, is, I, the, to, you, for, with,* and *in* are examples. In general, the more frequently a word occurs in English, the sooner students will need to be able to recognize it and spell it. This is one of the considerations taken into account when deciding at what grade level a word should be introduced. Commercial spelling lists, then, are made up of words students actually use in writing and words that occur frequently in print.

It makes good sense to teach children to spell the words they use most often in writing and see most often in their reading. However, many teachers find that the weekly spelling lists in spelling basals fall short of what they are looking for. There may not be enough examples of words that fit a particular pattern to help children master that pattern. Or words may be chosen to "fill out" a pattern but may not really be used by your students all that often. Many teachers want to *personalize* the words they present to students, to include the words a particular student or group consistently misspells week after week in writing, as well as words from math, science, health, social studies, and literature that will extend and enrich their students' writing. That is why the lists from spelling books just cannot fit everyone's needs.

In the sections that follow we will describe two basic methods of choosing words for spelling instruction: how to develop your own spelling lists, and how to adapt word lists from spelling basals.

Developing Your Own Spelling Lists

Some teachers prefer to develop their own lists of spelling words. If you do, there are several strategies you can employ that will help you.

Group words by patterns

First, words should be grouped by pattern. Patterns include letter patterns, such as the various ways to spell a long or short vowel sound, vowel digraphs such as *oi* and *oy,* and silent letter patterns; common prefixes or suffixes, such as words beginning with *re-, un-,* or *dis-* or ending with *-tion, -ily* or *-ment;* common base words or

roots and their derived forms; and meaning patterns, such as syn-
onyms and antonyms. Visual, sound, and meaning similarities are all
important patterns that children need to perceive.

Remember: *children learn to spell pattern by pattern, not word by
word*. Humans are naturally attuned to perceiving and making use of
patterns in all the information they take in and process. We look for
patterns, create hypotheses about other information that might fit the
same pattern, and act on these hypotheses. This is how human beings
learn. We do not learn to spell one word at a time. In spite of this,
some teachers create spelling lists that are simply collections of random words, usually selected from the story or topic being studied
that week. Faced with this kind of random collection of words,
children can do little except memorize. And it is brute memorization,
rather than real learning, that we are all trying to avoid in spelling
instruction. So it is very important to avoid simply creating a list of
words from a story, a science lesson, or the like without providing
some sort of pattern by which words can be grouped.

Sound and letter patterns. One useful way of organizing word lists
is by common sound patterns. We want children to have a body of
known words that share a common sound so that when they need to
write an unfamiliar word, they can relate it to familiar, known words
that sound the same way. That way, they may not always be right,
but they will come close.

Word families are a very useful vehicle for teaching common
sounds and familiarizing children with a group of words that have the
same pattern. Word families are groups of words that differ in beginning sound, but have the same vowel and ending sound and spelling;
for example, how many words can you think of that are spelled with
a consonant or blend plus *-at?* Stop reading now and jot down as
many *-at* words as you can on scrap paper, then count them up. Did
you come up with *at, hat, mat, sat, cat, that, fat, rat, drat, scat,* and even
a few more? Those words can be called "members of the *-at* family."
They make a great spelling list. Why? Because *-at* is a very common
pattern in English, and it makes up many common words that kids
are likely to encounter in their reading and want to use in their
writing. Familiarity with a pattern helps children be able to spell
other, unfamiliar words with the same pattern.

There are many other common sound patterns that may be
taught by word families. If you just start with short *a* patterns

you can quickly come up with -*ab*, -*ack*, -*at*, -*am*, -*an*, -*ad*, -*ast*, and others. Long *a* patterns include -*ade*, -*ace*, -*ate*, -*ame*, -*ane*, -*aid*, -*ain*, and others. Short *e* word families include -*en*, -*ed*, -*ess*, -*eck*, -*ell*, -*et*, and others; long *e* families include -*eet*, -*eep*, -*eel*, -*een*, -*ead*, -*eat*, -*ear*, and others. Short *i* patterns include -*ib*, -*in*, -*it*, -*ick*, -*ill*, -*iss*, -*id*, and so forth; long *i* patterns include -*ite*, -*ide*, -*ike*, -*ice*, -*ine*, and so forth. Short *o* families include -*ot*, -*ob*, -*on*, -*om*, and so forth; long *o* patterns include -*ope*, -*ote*, -*ose*, -*oke*, -*oat*, -*oar*, -*oak*, and so forth. Finally, short *u* families include -*up*, -*uss*, -*ug*, -*ud*, -*ut*, and -*un*; and long *u* families include -*ule*, -*uise*, and a few others. A representative list of word families is found in Table 7–1.

Word families are not the only sound features words have, although they make a convenient and memorable way to familiarize children with a lot of common words. Words can also be grouped together by their common beginning consonant blend or digraph sound (for example, words beginning with *th*-, or with *tr*- and *dr*-; or words beginning with or containing the "soft" sound of *c* as in *celery*). We don't need to belabor the point; word lists, especially for younger students, can and should be organized around sound, or phonetic features that words share. In chapter 6 we presented activities for teaching sound and letter relationships in words. You may also find Appendix B, which consists of word lists organized by sound features, helpful.

Visual patterns. Because children seem to "sound out" so much when they spell unfamiliar words, teachers often assume that the most important spelling patterns are sound patterns. However, our ability to spell depends as much on our ability to perceive and remember visual relationships among words. While sounding out is often helpful in trying to recognize an unfamiliar word in print, it may be less helpful in trying to produce, or spell, it. In spelling, the visual form of a correctly spelled word is the key to being able to spell it. Thus, patterns should be used that highlight the visual relations among words.

Therefore, another important strategy is to group words in lists according to visual patterns they have in common. For example, -*ough* is a common pattern in English that may sound differently in different words. But the pattern may be taught as a visual pattern, by grouping together words with the same spelling pattern but different sound patterns, such as *rough*, *tough*, *cough*, *enough*, *thought*, *fought*, *though*, and *through*.

TABLE 7–1   **Representative List of Word Families**

ab	aim	an	are	at
ace	ain	ance	ark	atch
ack	air	and	arm	ate
act	ait	ane	arn	ave
ad	ake	ang	arp	aw
ade	alk	ank	art	ax
aft	all	ant	ase	ay
ag	alt	ap	ash	aze
age	am	ape	ask	
aid	ame	ar	ass	
ail	amp	ard	ast	
ead	eat	een	elp	esk
eak	eck	eep	elt	ess
eal	ed	eer	em	est
eam	eed	eet	en	et
ean	eek	eg	end	etch
eap	eel	ell	ent	ew
ear	eem	elm	ep	
ib	ig	ince	irt	itch
ibe	ike	ind	is	ite
ick	ile	ine	ise	ive
id	ill	ink	ish	ix
ide	ilt	int	isk	ize
ife	im	ip	iss	izz
iff	ime	ipe	ist	
ift	in	ire	it	
oach	obe	oll	oop	orn
oad	ock	om	oor	ort
oak	od	ome	oot	ose
oal	ode	on	op	ot
oam	oft	one	ope	otch
oan	og	oof	or	ote
oap	oid	ook	orb	ow
oast	oil	ool	ord	owe
oat	oke	oom	ore	ox
ob	ole	oon	ork	oy
ub	ug	ume	ur	ush
ube	uge	un	ure	usk
uck	ule	und	urn	uss
ud	ull	une	urt	ust
ude	ult	unk	us	ut
uff	um	up	use	ute
				uzz

91

There are a number of other patterns that may be taught as visual patterns; double consonants, either at the end or in the middle of words, are another example. For example, here are words with *bb: babble, bubble, dabble, gobble, rabbit, ribbon, rubber,* and *wobble.* Here are words with *gg: egg, giggle, goggles, wiggle, waggle.* These words have *nn: annoy, banned, bunny, dinner, flannel, funnel, granny, minnow, penny, running, skinny,* and *tunnel.* You will find lists of words sharing the same letter feature in Appendix B.

Semantic, or meaning, patterns. Visual memory alone is not enough; meaning elements of words are also critically important. Word lists that include related forms of the same word, words with similar base words, and words that are related by meaning help children use their analytical reasoning, which helps the mature speller relate unknown words to known words. This is the ultimate strategy of the mature speller: the ability to figure out how to correctly spell an unknown word by relating it to similar, previously learned words. We help students learn to do this kind of thinking by organizing word lists that include important meaning relationships.

One strategy is to organize word lists so that we teach common structural patterns. For example, a structural pattern we teach fairly early is the formation of plurals: adding *s* to words not ending in *s,* as in *dogs, cats, cars, papers,* and *books;* adding *es* to words already ending in *s, ch,* or *sh,* as in *glasses, dishes, kisses, watches,* and so forth; and adding no ending but instead changing the base word's spelling in some irregular plurals, like *men, women, children, oxen, mice,* and *lice.* By the same strategy, we could group common verbs with their past and present verb forms: *walk, walks, walking, walked; drive, drives, driving, drove; write, writes, writing, wrote; amaze, amazes, amazing, amazed; bark, barks, barking, barked;* and so forth. Regular and irregular past tense forms could be contrasted.

Similarly, adding *-ment* to a verb creates a noun form, as in *amaze / amazement, encourage / encouragement, measure / measurement, entertain / entertainment,* and so forth. The suffix *-er* is added to many words to indicate "a person or thing that does": for example, a thing that washes dishes is a *dishwasher;* a person who writes is a *writer:* a thing that makes copies is a *copier. Teacher, reporter, manager, flier, runner, fighter, typewriter, seller,* and *buyer* are other examples of words that fit this pattern. The suffix *-tion* and its variations are added to verbs to make more nouns: *nation, vacation, collection, election, fraction,* and *pollution* are examples. Another way to organize word lists by semantic features is to group a base word and its derived forms that share a related meaning. For example, the Latin base *medica* is shared by *medical, medic, medicine, medicinal, medicate,* and *medication.* The Greek suffix *-scope* is shared by *telescope, microscope, horoscope,* and *periscope.* The Latin stem *scire,* meaning "to know," is shared by *science, scientist, scientific,* and *scientism.* Many other groups of related words can be generated without much effort: *critic, criticize,* and *criticism; express, expression, compress,* and *compression; sign, signal, signet, signature,* and *resign.* A helpful list of Greek and Latin stems and affixes is included in Appendix A.

Include words from content subjects and stories

Include words from content subjects and stories currently being read that fit the patterns you are working on. This helps students see that spelling is an integral part of the entire curriculum and embraces all the language arts. In this way, words are not studied in isolation but also in the context of literature, nonfiction, and subject-area lessons. Speaking and writing vocabularies are enhanced as children study words from other lessons as spelling words and see spelling words in their natural contexts. Examples of content-area words may be math words: *add, addition, subtract, subtraction, multiply, multiplication, divide, division, quotient, divisor, fraction;* science words: *species, habitat, environment, pollute, atmosphere;* weather words: *temperature, pressure, dewpoint, cloudy, thunder;* geometry words: *oval, trapezoid, rectangle, acute, angle, diameter;* and so forth.

Include commonly used words for review

You should also include as review words commonly used words that students often habitually misspell. Many students have consistent trouble spelling words like *these, which, about, too,* and many other words that occur frequently in reading and writing. They may continue to misspell these words long after they have progressed to correct spelling of much more difficult words. This may be in part because these "little words" are often not attended to very carefully in print, and also in part because of habit. In any event, periodic review of commonly used words helps all students, for they all need to use these words every day in their writing. Also, real learning is facilitated with periodic review.

Over the years several lists of commonly used words have been developed. When these lists are compared, it has been found that differences between lists are insignificant. The 500 words most frequently occurring in children's writing and the words most often misspelled in children's writing are given in Appendixes C and D.

Avoid uncommon or unusual spelling words

Avoid words that are unusual, uncommon, or unfamiliar even if they fit the particular pattern you're working on. Remember, you cannot teach students to spell all the words they may conceivably need in their writing; you can only teach a representative group, and the rules and strategies by which students may generalize the spelling of an unfamiliar word from a similar, known word. Stick to the most common exemplars of a pattern, and it is more likely that students will remember both it and the pattern. For unusual or uncommon words, teach them how to use a dictionary.

You can determine which words students consistently misspell in their written work by periodically reviewing students' writing folders. Keep a list of typical misspellings, and keep a tally of how many students seem to be making the same or similar mistakes. For example, a number of students may be failing to mark long vowels with silent *e* and misspelling a variety of long *e* words. These and similar words may be the basis for several spelling lessons on silent *e* and long *e*. Students may also be encouraged to keep an individual notebook or list of personal spelling "demons," words that an individual speller often has trouble with. You can periodically review these for particular patterns that are giving students problems.

Using Word Lists from Spelling Basals

Many teachers still use word lists provided by spelling basals but do not use the basal to teach them. But the same list may not be appropriate for all the students in your room.

Just as you probably have children working at different levels of proficiency in reading, you probably have children working at different levels of proficiency in spelling. The same book will not be appropriate for all the readers in your classroom; in the same way, the same spelling list will not fit all spellers. Children need to work at their instructional levels in spelling, just as they do in reading. The appropriate instructional spelling level is one where the child is working at a level of *comfortable challenge*. Neither too easy nor too hard, the words are, like Baby Bear's chair, "just right."

Therefore, in order to use basal lists you need to have several consecutive levels of the same spelling series, or graded word lists, available for your students. Each student should be given the pretest or diagnostic placement test that accompanies the series. If no placement test is available, follow this procedure for placing students at the appropriate level:

1. Make a twenty-word sample of the words at each spelling level. Choose five words from each quarter of the book; that is, five words from the first seven or eight lessons, five words from the second seven or eight lessons, and so forth.

2. Give all students the set of words for their present grade level. Those who spell between about 50 percent and 75 percent of the words correctly would be appropriately placed in that level. Those who spell 50 percent or fewer of the words should be tested in a lower level; those who spell 75 percent or more of the words correctly should be tested on a higher grade level. Repeat the placement testing at lower and higher levels until all students are placed.

Commercial spelling programs usually feature twenty or twenty-five words in each weekly lesson. If children are appropriately placed using the 50 percent to 75 percent criterion, a twenty-word list exposes a child to five to fifteen new words each week. This may be too many words for some of your students. In fact, it is better to have children learn fewer words and learn them reliably than to have them memorize more words and forget them or mix them up later! Depending on the grade, word lists of between six and twenty words are probably the right length. In the primary grades, word lists of four to six words for the average speller and as many as ten per lesson for the better speller are about right; for the middle elementary grades, use six to ten for poor spellers and ten to fifteen for better spellers; and in middle school plan on six to ten for poorer spellers and as many as twenty for better spellers.

As you can see there is much to consider when you help spellers develop and use word lists in the classroom. In the next chapter, we will broaden our view as we discuss how to implement and promote a schoolwide plan for developmental spelling instruction.

8

The Effective Schoolwide Spelling Curriculum

SPELLING IS OF such great importance it deserves schoolwide attention. An appropriate spelling curriculum must build upon existing knowledge and span the elementary years. It must involve the understanding and participation of parents as well as teachers. What we recommend is a schoolwide spelling program. If you are a teacher, parent, or administrator, you may wonder: How effective is my school's current spelling curriculum? How does my school's program measure up? To help you answer these questions we've developed the following checklist. The checklist is followed by an explanation of each criterion.

An effective schoolwide spelling program provides the following (you may wish to check each item that describes the program in your school):

1. Encouragement and appropriate response for invented spelling at early stages of development.
2. Developmentally appropriate word study, including word lists and a plan for providing continuous, developmental word study and spelling evaluation throughout the elementary school years.
3. Multilevel spelling instruction and resources in every classroom.
4. An observable plan for moving children out of the transitional level of invented spelling into formal or direct spelling instruction.
5. Use of visualization strategies to help further develop the visual coding mechanism.

6. A viable management system for instructional activities and assessment.
7. Appropriate aids to spelling.
8. An assessment component.
9. A plan to develop schoolwide spelling consciousness.
10. A parent education component.

Some existing schoolwide spelling programs that are fairly good address many of the criteria on our checklist. But *all ten components are needed* for an optimal spelling program. Our checklist is like a recipe: if you leave out any one ingredient, you may spoil what comes out. Let's look briefly at all ten criteria.

First of all, an effective schoolwide spelling program must value and encourage invented spelling as a natural means for building the foundation for spelling competence. There is no better way to develop early spelling consciousness and growth than to properly nurture inventive spellers. Allowing youngsters to invent spelling is the best way to get beginning spellers to think about spelling and to apply their knowledge of the alphabet and awareness of phonemes in meaningful and purposeful contexts. Invented spelling sets the foundation for later spelling competence.

Second, children must study words in order to learn to spell them. Expert spelling is not simply caught. An effective program provides a safety net to make sure that exposure to words and assessment of words is continuous and comprehensive throughout a child's elementary school experience. A hit-or-miss attitude is not good enough.

Third, learning to spell is a complex, individual accomplishment. Spelling must be individualized to be taught. It is not appropriate to have every child in the classroom memorizing the same list of words.

Fourth, there must be a plan for moving children from transitional spelling. A child's use of transitional spelling is a signal to the teacher that he or she is ready to look at words intensely and in specific ways in order to learn to spell them. Transitional spelling should signal the advent of formal spelling instruction.

Expert spelling is a highly visual skill that invokes the visual coding mechanism. Expert spellers install words in their visual memory. As children inspect words in order to learn to spell them, they must be shown strategies that will help them increase their capacity to store and retrieve words visually.

Next, a viable system of management must be in place. Classrooms run differently depending upon the management style of the teacher and the characteristics of the students. One particular management style doesn't necessarily work for everyone. What is important is that there be a plan for effective management. Classrooms—particularly those where various spelling activities are going on simultaneously—do not run effectively without forethought, organization, and management. We recommend management systems in which students take responsibility as collaborators. Encouraging a collaborative role in students helps them develop proper attitudes toward spelling and knowledge of themselves as competent word users and spellers.

Here are a few examples of classroom management alternatives:

1. Use a buddy system. Allow two students to team up each week to alternate administering the spelling survey (pretest) and the self-correction check (see chapter 6). Teams may also be used for visualization strategies, games, and other activities for practicing spelling words.

2. Use peer tutoring with a competitive twist. Divide the class in half, into two teams. The two teams compete for points where students in each team work in pairs or small groups. Teams get points and certificates for words correct in practice. Bonus points are earned for correct tutoring or use of techniques recommended by the teacher.

3. Use cooperative learning techniques. Encourage student participation in building teams, setting goals, measuring progress, establishing reward systems, and enhancing time on task and performance. Spelling practice is a great venue for cooperative learning. One objective of the spelling program should be that students become active collaborators in their own development.

Whatever the management system you adopt, however, remember that effective classroom management always includes practice and feedback, self-regulation, self-monitoring, and a sense of ownership of the process.

Another essential ingredient in an effective spelling program is the use of spelling aids. Students must have access to and experience in the use of dictionaries, thesauri, spelling games, and spell-checkers. Computers provide excellent spell-checkers. Hand-held spelling "calculators" are popular in many classrooms for helping students locate alternative spellings. Other spelling aids include wall charts, class demon lists, individual compilations of frequently misspelled words, and charts and graphs for recording progress.

Like classroom management techniques, good schoolwide spelling assessment can come in many varieties; but there are some constants. Assessment should be continuous and should monitor spelling growth throughout the elementary years. Students, parents, and teachers should have access to information regarding the student's growth as a speller. Traditional pencil-and-paper assessment has a place in a schoolwide spelling program, with spelling surveys (pretests) followed by word study and post-tests. Assessment should be enhanced by monitoring spelling in children's writing, conferencing, keeping records, and encouraging the compilation of portfolios for spelling. We favor assessment strategies that allow students themselves to set appropriate goals, monitor their own progress, keep records, and "test out" or recycle words until they learn them. Above all else, assessment for spelling should be a positive concept in the eyes of the student. The focus should be on accomplishment, with much less of the traditional emphasis on test grades.

In an effective spelling program, spelling consciousness is schoolwide. The school can take much responsibility in building positive spelling consciousness. Do students have accurate knowledge of themselves as spellers and a desire and concern for correct spelling in the appropriate contexts? Is the school helping them develop a habit of care for correct spelling? There are so many opportunities each school year to build spelling consciousness. It all begins with an acknowledgment that spelling is important.

Finally, parents must be enlisted to help. They may be involved in the schoolwide spelling program on many levels, but their involvement begins with the school's plan for parent education. Many parents have no understanding of the concept of invented spelling, for example. The traditional struggle at home to prepare for the weekly spelling test can lead to family crisis. The goal of parent education is twofold: to introduce parents to the curriculum so that they can help their sons and daughters develop as spellers; and to provide specific tips for how they might help. Parent education might include presentations or programs, letters to parents, and information shared in parent conferences. Don't underestimate parent education. Parents can be great allies in developing children who succeed as spellers.

At no time should we forget the relationship of spelling to writing. Spelling is critical in the writing process. We must lead children to value spelling as a tool for writing. We must lead them to make the spelling-writing connection. They must recognize that conventional spelling leads to competent writing.

Ultimately, spelling enables the writer to communicate with the minds of future generations. Have you read the writings of Benjamin Franklin, Mahatma Gandhi, Emily Dickinson, or Aristotle? What if Thomas Jefferson had not learned to spell? Jefferson, in fact, had a healthy personal regard for spelling. In a letter written to his daughter Patsy in 1783 he offered the following admonition: "Take care, that you never spell a word wrong. . . . It produces great praise to a lady to spell well" (quoted in Smith 1976, p. 171).

Attitudes have changed since Jefferson's time. Invented spelling has opened whole new avenues of expression for young people. Invented spelling frees the spirit to write things that otherwise might not be expressed. It empowers the incipient speller. We see this in a first grader's end-of-year letter to her teacher:

Dear Ms. Gowen

I've mist you sints the day we got out off school. You've been the best techere I've ever had. I want to tell you sumthing I lernd out off the *Holy Bible*. It came out off the Songs, Vers 23ed.

> the Lord is my sheperd
> I shal not want.
> He ledith me too lie down
> in the green pashtyou'rs.
> The Lord is a Lord off Love.

> Love
> Debbie!

We also see empowerment in the courageous invented spelling of a sixty-two-year-old who dares to use invented spelling to communicate, knowing full well that he has not mastered conventional spelling.

> Gon tu
> hoss spit all
> De parson is in Rume 294.

101

Isn't every educated citizen entitled to be taught spelling? Can we afford to make curricular decisions that will fail others as we have failed this sixty-two-year-old speller? Let's begin to treat spelling with integrity. We ask that you recognize the importance of spelling for the language learner. We ask that you go out and teach it.

Appendix A

Origins of English Words

---

140 Useful Latin Stems

Original Latin	Meaning	English Descendants
aequus	equal	equal, equality, equation, equator
agere	to drive, to act	act, agent, reaction, agile
ambulare	to walk	amble, ambulance, ambulatory
anima	spirit, breath	animal, animated, unanimous
aqua	water	aquatic, aqualung, aquarium, aqueduct
arma	arms	arms, armor, armored, armory, armament, army
audire	to hear	audition, auditorium, audience, obey
cadere	to fall	incident, occident (where the sun falls), accident, cascade, casual, occasion
caedere	to cut	suicide, homicide, decide, precise, scissors
caelum	heaven	ceiling, celestial
calere	to be hot	cauldron, calories, scald
campus	plain	camp, campaign, champion
candere	to shine	candid, candle, candidate, candor, chandelier, incandescent, kindle
cantare	to sing	chant, enchant, canticle, descant
capa	cape	chaperone, escape, chapel, cope, escapade
capere	seize, lay hold of, contain	accept, anticipate, capable, capsule, case, cash, casket, catch, chase,

Original Latin	Meaning	English Descendants
		concept, conceive, deceive, except, occupy, perceive, purchase, recipe
caput	head	captain, capital, cattle, chapter
causa	cause	cause, because, excuse, accuse
cedere	to come, to yield	recess, success, excess, cease, decease, access, ancestor, concede
circus	ring	circle, circus, research, search, shark
civis	citizen	city, civil, civilized, civilization, citizen
clamare	call out	claim, clamor, proclaim, exclaim
claudere	to close	enclose, include, claustrophobia, close, closet
cor	heart	courage, concord, discord, cordial, heart
corpus	body	corporal, corpulent, corps, corpse, corpuscle, incorporate
credere	to believe	credit, incredible, credence, creed, grant
crescere	to grow	crescent, concrete, decrease, increase, recruit
currere	to run	current, course, concourse, corridor, courier, cursive, occur, excursion
decire	to say	decide, dictate, contract, dedicate, dictionary, ditto, predicament, predict
ducere	to lead	produce, reduce, induce, educate, product, duct, duke
duo	two	dual, two, doubt, double, dozen, duel, dual, duplicate
errare	to stray	error, errand, erroneous
exter	outer	exterior, extra, strange, extraneous
facere (factus)	to do	fact, factory, facile, facilitate, feat, faculty, fashion, infect, perfect, defect, proficient, profit, sufficient, defeat, counterfeit
farire	to speak	fable, fairy, infant, infantry, confess
fendere	to strike	defense, fence, fend, offend
ferre	to bear	Christopher, circumstance, confer, infer, conference, prefer, refer, suffer
fingere	to fashion	fiction, figure, effigy, feign
finis	end	finish, final, finite, fine, refine, financial
flagere	to burn	flame, flamingo, flagrant, conflagration
flectere	to bend	reflect, deflect, flexible
fluere	to flow	influence, fluent, flow, fluctuate, fluid
fortis	strong	fort, fortify, fortitude, fortress
frangere	to break	fraction, fracture, fragile, fragment, refrain

Original Latin	Meaning	English Descendants
genus	kin	genuine, generate, genius, gentle, gentile, general
gradus	step	degree, graduate, gradual, progress, digress, regress, grade, degrade
gratus	pleasing	congratulate, agree, grace, grateful, ingrate
habere	to have	habit, inhabit, habitation, inhibit, prohibit
horrere	to bristle	horrify, horrible, abhor, horror
iacere (jacene)	to throw	inject, reject, jet, jettison, jetty, adjacent
iungere (jungere)	to join	junction, join, joint, injunction, conjunction
legere	to collect, to read	collect, elect, intelligent, elegant, eligible, lecture, legend, lesson, neglect, select
liber	free	liberal, liberty, liberation
littera	letter	literal, literature, literate, alliteration
magnus	great	magnificent, magnate, magistrate, main, magnify, majesty, mayor, master
mandare	to put in the hands of	command, demand, recommend
manus	hand	maintain, manage, manner, maneuver, manufacture
memoria	remembrance	memory, remember, memorial
migrare	to wander	migrate, immigrate, emigrate
minuere	to make smaller	minute, minus, minor, diminish
mirus	wonderful	admire, miracle, mirror, mirage, smile
mittere (miss-)	to send	transmit, missile, mission, emit, dismiss, omit, permit, promise, submit
monere	to advise	comment, demented, mental, mention, money, demonstrate, monster, monument, summon
movere	to move	emotion, mob, commotion, mobile, moment, motor, remove, promote
nocere	to hurt	innocent, obnoxious, noxious, nuisance
nomen	a name	ignore, noble, notice, notion, recognize
noscere	to get to know	ignore, noble, notice, notion, recognize
numerus	number	numerous, numeral, number
nuntius	messenger	announce, pronounce, denounce, nuncio
nutrire	nourish	nurse, nutrient, nutrition, nourish
oculus	eye	binocular, inoculate, canopy, monocle
ordo	order	ordinal, ordinary, order, ordain, subordinate

105

Original Latin	Meaning	English Descendants
pacere (pact)	to agree	Pacific, peace, pacify, appease, compact
pangere (pact-)	to bind	pact, dispatch, impact, impinge, page, pageant, pay
parare	to prepare	parade, prepare, compare, separate, several
pati (passi-)	to suffer	passion, passive, patient
pedem	foot	pedal, pedestrian, biped, impede, pawn, expedite, pedestal, pedigree, pioneer, impeach, tripod
pellere	to drive away	propeller, compel, impel, repel, repellant, pulse, push, repeal
planus	flat	plan, plain, plane, explain, plank
plenus	full	complete, accomplish, plenty, supply
ponere	to place	compound, deposit, opponent, opposite, positive, purpose
populus	people	people, popular, population, populace, public, publish
portare	to carry	portable, port, porter, export, import, important, report, sport
premere	to press	compress, depress, express, imprint, oppress, print
pretium	price	appreciate, prize, price, precious, praise
primus	first	prime, prince, principal, primitive, prior
privus	single	private, privilege, deprive
probus	good	prove, approve, probably
proprius	one's own	appropriate, proper, property, propriety
pungere	to prick	punctuation, punch, point, pounce, punctual
quattuor	four	quadruple, quadruped, squad, square
quietus	at rest	quit, quiet, acquiesce, quite, requiem
quoerere (quoest-)	to seek	request, require, inquisition, quest, question
radere (rase-)	to scrape	erase, rascal, rash, razor
regere	to rule	correct, direct, dress, real, realm, rectangle, regal, regent, regiment, regular, reign, resource, rule
rodere	to gnaw	rodent, corrode, erode
rumpere (rupt)	to break	abrupt, corrupt, disrupt, interrupt, erupt, rupture
sal	salt	salt, salary, salad, sauce, sausage
scandere	to climb	ascend, descend, scale, scan, scandal
scire	to know	conscience, conscious, science
scribere	to write	script, describe, scripture, scribble, subscribe

106

Original Latin	Meaning	English Descendants
secare	to cut	insect, disect, intersect, section, segment
sedere	to sit	session, sediment, sedentary, size, subside, settle
sentire	to feel	sense, scent, sentence, resent, sentiment, sensory
sequi (secut–)	to follow	consecutive, consequence, second, execute, pursue, sect
serere	to join	assert, concert, desert, insert, series, exert
signum	a sign	signal, signature, resign, design, ensign, insignia
similis	like	similar, similarity
simul	together	assemble, simultaneous, resemble, same
socius	a follower	society, social, sociable
solidus	solid	solid, soldier, consolidate
solus	alone	solitary, sole, solitude, solo
solvere	to loosen	solve, dissolve, resolve
sonus	sound	consonant, parson, person, sound, unison
sors (sort–)	lot	assorted, resort, consort, sort
spectare	to look	respect, aspect, inspect, despise, despite, special, species, perspective, specify, spectator, spectacular, spy, suspect, suspicion
sperare	to hope	desperate, despair, prosper
spirare	to breathe	inspire, perspire, conspire, spirit, sprite
spondere	to promise	correspond, sponsor, spouse, respond, despondent
stare (stat–, sist–)	to stand	station, stable, statue, static, stage, establish, substitute, subsist, status, insist, resist
staurare	to set up	store, story (as in a house), restaurant, restore
sternere (strat–)	to strew	stray, street, straw
stringere (strict–)	to draw tight	district, restrict, constrict, strict, string
struere (struct–)	to build up	instruct, destruction, construct, construe
super	above	supervise, superman, super
tangere (tag–, tact–)	to touch	tag, contact, taste, task, tax
tegere (tect–)	to cover	detect, protect, tectonics
tempus	time	temporary, tense
tendere	to hold out or stretch out	tent, tender, tendon, extend, contend, pretend

Original Latin	Meaning	English Descendants
tenere	to hold	contain, content, continent, continue, tempt, entertain, tenant, maintain
terra	earth	terra-cotta, terrain, terrestrial, terrier, territory
textere	to weave	text, context, tissue, textile
torquere (tort-)	to twist	torture, tortoise, extort, torment, torch
trahere (tract-)	to draw	trace, retreat, train, trait, treat, treaty, portrait, tractor, tract, contract, distract, retract
tres	three	triple, tripod, treble, triangle, trillion, trio, trivial
unus	one	unite, unify, uniform, union, unit, unique
vadere	to go	invade, wade, evade
valere	to be strong	valid, value, valiant, prevail, convalesce
venire (vent-)	to come	avenue, prevent, invent, vent, convenient
verbum	word	adverb, verbal, verb, proverb
vertere	to turn	invert, revert, vertebra, divert, reverse, inverse, conversion
verus	true	verdict, verify, very
videre	to see	vision, advise, evident, provide, review, view, survey, visit, wise, wit
vivere (vict-)	to live	revive, survive, convivial, victuals, vital, vivid
volvere (volut-)	to roll	revolve, involve, revolt, vault, volume
vox (voc-)	voice	vocal, provoke, voice, vowel

42 Useful Prefixes from Latin, Greek, and English

Prefix	Meaning	Prefix	Meaning
a-	not	hypo-	under
ab-	away from	in-	into
ad-	to, toward	in-	not
ambi-	both	inter-	between
amphi-	both	intra-	within
anti-	against	juxta-	hear
auto-	self	mis-	badly
bi-	double	mono-	double
cata-	down, downwards	multi-	many
circum-	around	non-	not
com-, con-	with, together	ob-, o-	near
contra-	against	per-	through

Prefix	Meaning	Prefix	Meaning
de-, dis–	un	peri-	around
dia–	through, between	poly-	many
		pre-	before
dis-	apart, away	pro-	before, instead of
duo-	double	proto-	first
dys-	badly	re-	again
en-	in	retro-	backwards
epi-	upon	semi-	half
ex-	out of, away	sub-	under
extra-	beyond	super-	above
fore-	before	syn-	with, together with
hetero-	other	trans-	beyond
holo-	whole, entire	tri-	thrice
hyper-	above, beyond	un-	not

25 Useful Greek Stems

Original Greek	Meaning	English Descendants
arche	a beginning	anarchy, archaeology, architect, archive, monarch
aster	a star	asterisk, asteroid, astronomy, disaster, astrology
bios	life	amphibious, biography
bombos	a humming	bomb, bombard, bump, boom
burse	a hide	purse, bursor, reimburse
chronos	time	chronology, synchrony
ergon	work	ergonomics, energy, organ
geo	earth	geology, geography
graph	to write	autograph, photograph, biography
helios	sun	helium, heliocentric
hydris	water	hydro-, hydrogen
klin	to lean or slope	incline, decline, climate
kratus	strong	democracy, aristocracy, autocracy
krin	to judge	critic, crisis, criterion
kentron	a spike	center, eccentric, centrifugal
logos	a saying, to speak	analogy, apology, catalogue, logic, dialogue, -logy
metron	a measure	diameter, meter, perimeter, symmetry, barometer
monos	single	monarch, monastery, monk, monopoly, mono
pathos	suffering	sympathy, pathetic, apathy

Original Greek	Meaning	English Descendants
petros	stove	petroleum, petrify, pier
phone	sound	phonetic, symphony, telephone
poene	penalty	punish, impunity, penal, penitent, repent, subpoena
skep, scop	I consider	skeptic, scope
theao	I see	theater, theory, ampitheater
tonos	a tone	tone, tune, monotone, tonic

Appendix B

Word Lists Organized
by Sound or Letter

Initial Consonants

b

baboon baby back bacon
bad badge bag bait ball
ballet balloon banana bar
bark barn basket bass bat
bath bear bed been bell
bend berry best bib bicycle
big bike bird board boat
bone bonus bottle box
bubble buffalo builder
bulletin bunny bus butter
button buy

hard c

cab cabinet cactus cage cake
calf call came camel camera
camp canary candle candy
cane card carrot cast castle
cave canter cob coin cold
comb come comic continent
continue cook cork corn
count cousin cow cub
cup cut

soft c

cease cedar ceiling celery cell
cellar cement censor census
cent center central ceramic
cereal certain cider cinema
cinnamon circle circus cite
citizen citrus city civil cycle
cyclone cylinder cymbal

d

dab dad damp dance dark
dart dash date day dead
deal dear den dent dentist
desk dice did diet dill
dime dimple dinosaur dip
dirty disc dish dive divide

do   doctor   does   dog   doll
dollar   domino   done   donkey
donut   door   dot   double
down   duel   dug   dull   dummy
duplicate   dust

f
face   fact   faith   fall   family
fan   fantastic   far   farm   farmer
farther   fast   fat   fear   fed
feet   fence   fiddle   fifteen   fig
fill   fin   find   finger   fire   first
fish   fit   five   fix   flag   food
foot   for   fork   forty   foul
found   fourteen   fox   fudge
full   fume   funny

hard g
gab   gag   gain   gallon   gamble
game   garbage   garden   gas
gate   gave   gear   gallant
gadget   gable   gallop   gift   gig
girl   give   go   goat   goblin
goes   gold   gone   good   gopher
gorilla   got   gut

soft g
gee   gel   gelatin   Gemini
gender   gene   general   genetics
gens   gentle   gentry   giant
gibber   gibe   gigantic   gin
ginger   giraffe   gist   gym   gyp
gypsy

h
hack   had   hail   half   hallow
ham   hammer   hammock   hand
hard   has   hat   hatch   have
hay   he   head   hear   heart
hedge   help   hem   hen   her
here   hid   hide   high   hill

hinge   hip   hippo   hit   hockey
hog   hold   holiday   home
hook   hoop   hop   hope   horn
horse   house   hug   human
humming   hurt   husband   hut

j
jabber   jack   jacket   jag   jail
jam   jar   jaw   jazz   jeans   jeep
jelly   jet   jewel   jiffy   jiggle
jitter   job   jog   join   joke
jolly   jolt   joy   judge   judo
juggle   juice   jumble   jumbo
jump   June   jungle   junk
jury   just

k
kale   kangaroo   karate   keel
keen   keep   keg   kennel   kept
kernel   ketchup   kettle   key
kick   kid   kidnap   kill   kiln
kilo   kilt   kind   kindle   king
kink   kiss   kite   kitty   kiwi
koala

l
lab   label   labor   lace   lack
lad   ladder   ladybug   lag   lake
lamb   lamp   land   lantern   lap
large   last   late   laugh   lavatory
leaf   lean   leap   leave   led   leg
lemon   leopard   let   letter
lettuce   lick   lid   life   lift
light   like   lily   limb   lime
limp   line   lion   lip   list   lit
litter   little   live   lizard   llama
load   loaf   loan   lobby   lobster
local   locker   lofty   log   loin
lone   long   look   loon   loop
lot   love   low   lucky   lug
lumpy   lunch   lung   lurk

m

machine   mad   made   magic
magician   magnet   mail   mailman
main   man   mantle   many   map
march   mare   mars   mask   mat
match   math   may   me   mean
meat   melon   men   mend
mercury   mere   merry   met
metal   mice   mid   middle   milk
mirror   mist   mix   mold   mole
mom   money   monkey   mood
moon   moose   mop   moral
moth   mother   mountain   mouse
mouth   much   mud   mug
munch   muscle   mushroom
music   mustache   my

n

nab   nag   nail   name   nap
napkin   narrow   nasty   nation
nature   naval   navy   near   neat
neck   necklace   need   needle
nerve   nest   net   never   new
newspaper   next   nibble   nice
nick   nickel   niece   night
nimble   nine   nip   no   noble
noise   noon   north   nose   not
notion   note   noun   now
number   nun   nurse   nut

p

pace   pack   pad   page   paid
pail   pain   paint   pajamas   palm
pan   panda   panther   paper
parade   park   parrot   party
pass   pasta   paste   pat   patch
paw   peach   peanut   pear   peg
pen   penny   people   pepper
period   pet   piano   pickle
picnic   picture   pie   pig   pillow
pin   pink   pint   pipe   pit
pizza   pocket   poem   poetry

point   poke   pole   police   pony
poodle   popcorn   pull   pumpkin
pupil   puppy   purple   purse
puzzle

q

quack   quail   quake   quarrel
quart   quarter   queen   question
quick   quiet   quilt   quip   quit
quite

r

rabbit   raccoon   race   rack
radio   radish   raft   rag   rail
rainbow   raincoat   raisin   rake
ram   ran   ranch   range   rank
rap   rare   rat   rate   rattle
read   ready   rear   reason   red
reindeer   remainder   rent   report
rest   rib   rid   ride   rig   right
rim   ring   rip   river   road
roam   rob   robe   robot   rocket
roller   rooster   root   rose   rot
round   routine   row   rub
rubber   rug   ruler   rum   run
rust

s

sack   sad   safe   sag   said   sail
sailor   sake   salt   same   sample
sand   sandwich   sang   sap   sat
satin   sauce   save   savor   saw
say   sea   seal   seam   search
seasonal   seat   second   seed
seek   seesaw   self   sell   sent
sentence   serve   set   seven   sick
side   sign   signal   sing   sister
sit   six   so   soap   sob   sock
soda   soft   some   soon   sound
soup   south   sub   subtract   suit
sum   sun   sunny   super   supper

t

tab table tack tag tail take
tale tall tame tan tank tap
tape tar taste tax taxi tea
teacher team tear tease teddy
teepee telephone tell ten
tennis tent test tide tie
tiger tight tile tilt time tin
title toad toast today toe
together told tomorrow too
took tool tooth top tot
toy tuba tug tumble turkey
turn turtle tutor tux

v

vacuum vail valentine valid
valley value van vary vase
vault veil velvet verb very
vest veto vice view villa
vine violet violin virus visit
vital vivid vocal voice void
volcano volley volt vote
vulture

w

wag wagon waist wait wake
walk wall wallet walrus
wand wane want war warm
was wash watch water
watermelon wave wax way
wear weasel web wed wee
weekday weld well went
were wet wig wild wildcat
will win windmill window
wish wit witch wolf woman
wood wool word work
worm would

x

xylophone

y

yak yammer yang yank yap
yard yarn yawn yea year
yeast yell yellow yen yes
yet yield yo-yo yoga yogurt
yolk yonder you young
your yummy

z

zany zap zeal zebra zenith
zero zesty zig-zag zinc
zipper zippy zither zombie
zone zoo

Initial Consonant Blends

bl

blab black blackboard blacken
blackout blame bland blank
blanket blare blaze bleach
bleak bleed blemish blend
blessed blight blimp blink
blip bliss blister blizzard
blob block blond blood
bloom blossom blot blouse
blow blubber blue blueberry
bluejay bluff blunt blush
bluster

cl

clack clad claim clam
clamber clamp clan clang
clank clap clarinet clarity
clash clasp class clatter claw
clay clean clear clench clerk
clever click client cliff
climate climb clinic clink clip
cloak clobber clock clod clog
clone clop close closet clothes
cloudy clout clown club clue
clumsy cluster clutch

fl

flabby   flag   flaky   flair   flank
flannel   flap   flare   flash   flask
flat   flatter   flaunt   flavor   flea
fleck   flee   fleece   fleet   flesh
flew   flex   flick   flicker   flier
flies   flight   flimsy   flinch   fling
flint   flip   flipper   flirt   flit
float   flock   flood   floor   flop
floppy   floral   flour   flow
flower   flown

gl

glacial   glacier   glad   glade
glamor   glance   gland   glare
glass   glaze   gleam   glee   glen
glib   glide   glider   glimmer
glimpse   glint   glisten   glitch
glitter   gloat   glob   global
globe   gloomy   glorify   glory
gloss   glove   glow   glue   glum

pl

place   placement   placid   plague
plaid   plain   plan   plane   planet
plank   plant   plantation   plaque
plaster   plastic   plate   plateau
platform   platoon   platter   play
plaza   plea   pleasant   please
pleasure   pleat   pledge   plenty
pliers   plight   plod   plop   plot
plow   pluck   plug   plumber
plummet   plump   plunder
plunger   plunk   plural   plus
plush   ply

br

brace   bracelet   brag   braid
braille   brain   bran   branch
brand   brash   brass   brave

bravo   brawl   bray   bread
breakfast   breast   breath   breeze
brew   bribe   brick   bridal
bride   bridge   brief   brilliant
bring   brisk   brittle   broad
broccoli   brochure   broil   broke
bronco   bronze   brook   broom
broth   brother   brought   brow
brown   brownie   bruise   brunch
brush   brutal   brute

cr

crab   crack   crackle   cradle
craft   crafty   cram   cramp
crane   crank   crash   crate   crave
crawl   crayon   crazy   creak
crease   create   creative   credit
creep   crept   crevice   crew   crib
cricket   cried   crime   criminal
crimp   cringe   crinkle   cripple
crisis   crisp   critic   crocodile
crook   crop   cross   crow
crowd   crown   crumb

dr

draft   drag   dragon   drain
dramatic   drank   drape   drapery
drastic   draw   drawer   drawl
dread   dream   dreary   dredge
dress   drew   drier   drift   drill
drink   drip   drive   drool   droop
drop   drought   drove   drowsy
drug   drum   drunk

fr

fraction   fracture   fragile
fragment   frail   frame   freckle
free   freedom   freeway   freeze
freight   frenzy   fresh   freshman
fret   friction   friend   fright

frigid   frisk   frivolous   frog
frolic   from   front   frosting
frown   frozen   frugal   fruit

gr

grab   grace   gracious   grade
graduate   grain   gram   grammar
grandfather   granola   grant
grape   grass   grate   grave
gravel   gravity   gray   grease
great   greed   green   greet   grew
grey   grid   grief   grieve   grin
grind   gristle   grit   groan
grocery   groom   gross   grouch
ground   group   grove   grow
gruff   grumpy   grunt

pr

practice   prairie   praise   prance
prank   preach   precede   precise
preen   president   press   pressure
pretend   pretty   prevent   price
pride   prim   primary   prime
primp   prince   princess   principal
print   prior   prize   produce
program   prom   promise
prompt   prong   proof   proper
protect   protein   protest   proud
provoke

tr

trace   track   tractor   trade
tradition   trail   trailer   train
trait   trample   trance   trap
trapeze   trash   travel   tray   treat
treaty   tree   tremor   triangle
tribe   tribute   trick   trickle
tricky   trifle   trigger   trim
trinket   trip   troll   troop
trophy   tropic   trot   trouble
true   trumpet   trunk   trust
truth

sc

scab   scald   scale   scallop   scalp
scamper   scan   scant   scar   scarf
scarlet   scary   scatter   scavenger
scold   scope   scorch   score
scorn   scorpion   scout   scowl
scuff   sculpt   scurry

scr

scrabble   scrap   scrape   scratch
scream   screech   screen   screw
scribe   scrimp   script   scrod
scroll   scrub   scruff   scrumptious

sm

small   smart   smash   smatter
smear   smell   smelt   smile
smirk   smite   smith   smock
smog   smoke   smoky   smolder
smooth   smother

sn

snack   snaffle   snafu   snag   snail
snake   snap   snare   snarl   snatch
sneak   sneer   sneeze   snicker
sniff   sniffle   snip   snipe   snob
snook   snoop   snoot   snooze
snore   snorkel   snort   snout
snow   snubby   snuff   snug
snuggle

sp

spa   space   spacious   spackle
spade   spaghetti   spall   span
spangle   spaniel   spank   spanner
spar   spare   spark   sparkle
sparrow   sparse   spasm   spat
spatter   spatula   spawn   spay
speak   spear   special   species
specific   specify   specious   speck
spectrum   speech   speed   spell

116

spend   spent   spice   spider
spike   spill   spin   spinach
spindle   spine   spinner   spiral
spirit   spit   spoil   sponge   spoof
spooky   spool   spoon   sport
spot   spur

spr

sprain   sprat   sprawl   spray
spread   spree   sprig   spring
sprinkle   sprint   sprocket   sprout
spruce   sprung

st

stab   stable   stack   stadium
staff   stag   stage   stagger   stain
stair   stake   stale   stalk   stall
stallion   stammer   stamp   stance
stand   standard   stanza   staple
star   starch   stare   stark   start
starve   stash   state   static
station   statue   status   stave
stay   steady   steak   steal   steam
steed   steep   steer   stem   stencil
step   stick   stiff   still   sting
stink   stint   stir   stock   stomach
stone   stoop   stop   storage
stork   storm   story   stout
stove   student   studio   study
stuff   stumble   stump   stupid

str

straddle   strafe   straggle   straight
strain   strait   strake   strand
stranger   strap   strategy   strath
straw   stray   streak   stream
street   strength   strenuous   stress
stretch   strew   strick   strickle
strict   stride   strike   string
strip   stripe   strive   strobe
stroke   stroll   stroller   strong

stroud   strove   struck   structural
struggle   strung   strut

sw

swab   swaddle   swag   swallow
swam   swamp   swan   swank
swap   swarm   swash   swat
sway   swear   sweat   sweep
sweet   swell   swelter   swerve
swift   swig   swim   swindle
swine   swing   swipe   swirl
swish   switch   swivel   swizzle
swoon   swoop   swop   sword
sworn   swum

tw

twaddle   twain   twang   tweed
tweezer   twelve   twenty   twice
twiddle   twig   twilight   twill
twin   twine   twinge   twinkle
twirl   twist   twit   twitch
twitter   twixt

Final Consonant Blends

-ft
cleft   draft   left   raft

-ld
bald   bold   build   child   cold
could   field   fold   gold   held
hold   mild   mold   old   should
sold   told   weld   wild   world

-lt
belt   delta   fault   felt   malt
melt   salt   welt

-mp
bump   camp   champ   clump
cramp   damp   dump   hump

jump lamp lump plump
pump rump stamp stump
thump tramp trump

-nd

around background band
behind bend bind blind end
find found friend grand
hand kind land lend mount
pond pound round sand
second send sound spend
stand understand

-nt

ant aunt bent front pent
plant rent sent tent went

-sk

ask brisk desk dusk husk
mask mollusk musk risk
task tusk

-st

artist beast best boast
breakfast breast cast chest
coast crest cyst digest fast
feast first fist forest jest
just last list most must
nest past pest post rest
roast test toast trust

Initial Consonant Digraphs

ch/ch/

chafe chaff chain chair
chalice chalk challenge
chamber champ chance change
channel chant chap chapter
charcoal charge chariot charity
charm chart chase chat
cheap cheat check checker
cheddar cheek cheep cheer
cheese cherish cherry chest

chew chick chicken chide
chief child chili chill chime
chimney chimp chimpanzee
chin chirp chive chocolate
choice choke chop chore
chow chuck chunk church
churn

ch/sh/

chagrin chaise chalet chandelier
chaparral chapeau charlotte
chateau chauffeur chef chemise
chevron chic chiffon chivalry
chute

ch/k/

chameleon chanter chaos
character charisma chemical
chemist chorale chord
chiropractor choir cholesterol
choral

ph/f/

phantom phase pheasant phew
philander phobia phoney photo
physics

sh

shabby shack shackle shad
shade shadow shaft shag
shake shale shall shallow
sham shame shampoo
shamrock shank shape shapely
share shark sharp shatter
shave shawl she shear shed
sheep sheet shelf shell sheriff
shield shift shin ship shirk
shirt shiver shoal shock shoe
shone shook shop short shot
shout shove shovel show
shuck shudder shun shut
shuttle shy

118

th   (voiced)

than	that	the	thee	their
them	then	thence	there	these
they	thine	this	those	thou
though	thus	thyself		

th   (unvoiced)

thank	thatch	thaw	theater
theft	theme	theory	thermos
thick	thicket	thief	thigh
thimble	thin	thing	think
third	thirsty	thirty	thistle
thong	thorn	though	thousand
thud	thug	thumb	thump
thunder			

wh/hw/

whack	whale	wham	whammy
whang	wharf	what	wheat
wheel	wheeze	when	where
whether	whey	which	whiff
while	whim	whimper	
whimsical	whip	whirl	whisk
whisker	whisper	whit	white
whittle	whiz	whoops	whopper

Final Consonant Digraphs

-ch

approach	attach	beach	bench
birch	branch	breach	bullfinch
bunch	clench	church	clinch
coach	detach	drench	each
enrich	finch	grinch	inch
leach	lunch	lurch	march
mulch	ostrich	ouch	peach
pinch	poach	punch	rich
search	such	teach	torch
touch			

-ck

aback	attack	barrack	beck
black	block	brick	buck

check	chuck	clack	click	
clock	cluck	cock	crack	deck
dock	duck	flack	fleck	flick
flock	hick	hock	jack	kick
knack	lack	lick	lock	luck
mock	neck	nick	o'clock	
pack	peck	pick	pluck	prick
quack	rack	rock	shack	slick
snack	sock	tack	tick	track
rick	whack	wick		

-ng

aging	among	bang	belong
bending	bing	ding	doing
fang	flung	gang	glazing
gong	hang	hung	oblong
pang	pasting	ping	prolong
prong	rang	ring	sang	sing
sling	song	strong	strung
stung	sung	swing	tang
teasing	thong	throng	turning
twang	unstrung	wing	wrung
zing			

-sh

ambush	anguish	ash	astonish
bash	blush	brandish	brush
bush	cash	clash	crush	dish
establish	famish	fish	flash
flush	fresh	gnash	gush	harsh
hush	lush	mash	mesh	plush
push	rash	rush	sash	smash
stash	trash		

Two Similar Silent Consonants

bb

babble	bubble	dabble	ebb
gobble	hobby	rabbit	ribbon
rubber	wobble		

cc

acclaim	accord	accumulate
occasion	occupy	occur	raccoon

dd
add   caddy   daddy   forbidden
griddle   hidden   ladder   middle
odd   paddle   puddle   saddle
sudden

ff
affair   bluff   buff   coffee   cuff
differ   efface   effect   effort   fluff
giraffe   huff   jiffy   off   offend
offer   puff   ruff   scuff   sheriff
sluff   snuff   whiff

gg
egg   gaggle   giggle   goggle
waggle   wiggle

ll
all   alloy   balloon   bell   belly
bill   call   cell   collect   dell
doll   dollar   ellipse   fellow
follow   gallon   gallop   hello
lollipop   lullaby   million   pill
roll   silly   skillet   small   spell
swallow   thrill   village   wall
yell   yellow

mm
ammonia   bummed   common
crammed   dimmer   drummer
glimmer   grammar   hammer
hammock   mammal   shimmer
slamming   slimmest   summer
trimmer   tummy

nn
annex   annoy   annual   banned
bunny   dinner   flannel   funnel
granny   minnow   nanny   penny
running   skinny   tunnel

pp
apparatus   apparel   appeal   apple
floppy   happen   happy   hippo
opponent   pepper   puppet
slipper   whipped   zipper

rr
arraign   array   arrest   arrive
arrogant   arrow   barrel   berry
carrot   cherry   ferry   merry
mirror   parrot   squirrel

ss
across   bass   bliss   boss   brass
chess   class   cross   dress   floss
fuss   glass   gloss   hiss   kiss
loss   mass   massage   message
pass   possible   press   scissors
stress   tassel

tt
attain   batter   better   bottom
butter   button   cotton   cutter
flatter   kitten   letter   litter   little
mitten   pretty   rattle   tattle

Silent Consonant Combinations

dg(e)
badge   bridge   budge   dodge
edge   fudge   hedge   judge
ledge   lodge   midget   nudge
pledge   ridge   sledge   wedge

(i)gh
blight   bright   fight   flight
fright   height   light   might
night   right   sigh   slight   tight

kn
knack   knave   knead   knee
knew   knickers   knife   knight

knit   knob   knock   knoll   knot
know   knowledge   knuckle

lm

alm   balm   calm   elm   embalm
palm   qualm   realm

mb

bomb   climb   comb   crumb
dumb   lamb   limb   numb
plumb   thumb

tch

batch   catch   ditch   dutch   fetch
hatch   hatchet   hitch   hutch
latch   match   notch   patch
pitch   watch   witch

Vowel Digraphs

ai

aid   bait   bail   braid   chain
daily   fail   faint   faith   frail
gain   gait   grain   hail   jail
laid   lain   maid   mail   nail
paid   pail   pain   paint   quail
raid   rail   rain   raise   raisin
sail   saint   stain   tail   taint
train   vain   wail   wait

ay

bay   bayonet   bray   cay   clay
day   daylight   delay   fay   fray
gray   hay   jay   lay   layer
may   nay   parlay   pay   play
ray   relay   say   slay   spay
stay   stray   tray   way

ea (reach)

beach   beacon   bead   beagle
beak   beam   bean   beast   bleach
breach   cheap   clean   deacon

each   feast   feat   gear   glean
heal   heap   heat   leaf   leak
leap   lease   leave   meal   mean
measles   meat   neat   peach
peal   peat   please   reach   read
real   ream   reason   sea   seal
seam   season   seat   steal   tea
teach   team   veal   weak   weasel
wheat

ea (weather)

breakfast   cleanser   dead   deaf
feather   head   health   heather
heaven   heavy   lead   leather
meadow   measure   pleasure
spread   sweater   thread   treasure
wealth   weapon   weather

ee

agree   beef   beep   beetle   cheek
cheese   deed   deem   deep   eel
feet   fleet   geese   heel   jeep
keen   keep   leek   meed   meek
needle   peek   peep   queen   reef
reel   seed   seek   seem   seen
seep   seethe   sheep   sleep
speech   speed   steep   sweet
teem   teeny   wee   weed   week
weep

ei (freight)

beige   eight   lei   neigh
neighbor   reign   reindeer   sleigh
weigh   weight

ei (ceiling)

ceiling   conceive   deify   either
leisure   neither   perceive   receipt
receive   seize   sheik   veil

ie (piece)

achieve   belief   chief   diesel

field   fiend   grief   grieve
hacienda   julienne   lief   lien
medieval   niece   obedient   piece
pier   prairie   siege   siesta   thief
thievish   wield   yield

oa

approach   boast   boat   broach
cloak   coach   coal   coast   coat
coax   croak   float   foam   gloat
goad   goal   goat   groan   load
loaf   loan   moan   moat   oaf
oak   oat   poach   roach   road
roam   roast   soak   soap   throat
toad   toast

oo (look)

book   brook   cook   cookie
crooked   dogwood   foot   good
goody   gook   hood   hoof
hook   look   misunderstood   nook
rookie   shook   soot   stood
took   whoop   wood

oo (spoon)

baboon   balloon   bamboo   bloom
blooper   boom   boon   boost
booth   booze   brood   broom
caboose   cartoon   coo   cool
coon   coop   droop   food
foolish   goober   goose   groove
hoop   hoot   igloo   kangaroo
loom   loon   loop   looser   loot
maroon   mood   moon   moose
mushroom   noodle   noose
pooch   poodle   pool   raccoon
roof   rooster   root   saloon
scoop   shampoo   shoot   smooth
spool   spoon   stool   tool   tooth
zoo

ou (rough)

cousin   curious   double

enormous   enough   envious
tough   trouble   young

ow (row)

arrow   below   billow   blow
blown   bowl   crow   elbow
fellow   flow   follow   glow
grow   harrow   known   low
mellow   mow   owe   owing
own   pillow   row   show   slow
snow   sorrow   sow   stow
swallow   throw   thrown
tomorrow   tow   willow

Vowel Diphthongs

au (Paul)

applause   auburn   audio   audit
auger   augment   au gratin
august   aunt   aura   auspice
austere   authentic   author   auto
autumn   caught   cauldron   caulk
cause   caustic   clause   daughter
daunt   dauphin   faucet   fault
faun   fraud   gaudy   gauze   haul
haunt   laud   launch   launder
laurel   maudlin   mauve   naughty
pauper   pause   sauce   saucer
taught   vault

aw(saw)

awe   awful   awkward   bawl
brawl   caw   claw   crawl   dawn
draw   drawer   drawn   fawn
flaw   hawk   hawthorn   jaw
law   lawn   lawyer   mohawk
paw   pawl   pawn   raw   saw
shawl   slaw   sprawl   straw
tawny   thaw   yawn

all (fall)

all   allspice   ball   ballplayer   call
callable   fall   fallout   gall   hall

hallway install mall pall
small spall squall stall tall
tallest wall walled wallet

joy loyal ploy royal soy
toy voyage

ew (new)

anew askew blew brew
chew clew crew dew drew
few flew grew hew hewn
jewel knew new newly
news newscaster pew renew
screw shrew shrewd skew
spew stew threw view
whew yew

ou (pout)

about account aloud amount
announce blouse bounce bound
cloud clout couch count
crouch devour doubt flour
flout foul found ground
grout hound hour house
loud mound mount mouse
mouth noun ouch ounce our
out pouch pound pout
proud round scour scout
shout sour sprout thou
trounce trout

oi (coil)

anoint appoint asteroid avoid
boil boisterous broil choice
coil coin despoil foible foil
hoist join joist loin loiter
moist noise oil point poise
poison soil toil turmoil
voice void

ow (how)

allow brow brown chow
clown cow crowd crown
dower down drown endow
flower fowl gown grown how
howl jowl now owl plow
pow powder power prow
prowl rowdy scow shower
town vow vowel wow

oy (toy)

ahoy alloy annoy boy
convoy decoy destroyer
disloyal employ enjoy hoy

Appendix C

Five Hundred Words Most Frequently Used in Children's Writing

(Arranged in groups of ten, from 1 to 500. The first group (A to HE) lists the *most* frequently used words and the last group (BELIEVE to BECOME) lists the *least* frequently used.)

a	for	with	his
the	you	had	about
and	she	are	
I		so	
to		went	day
was	be	up	out
my	on	at	him
of	but	said	will
we	when		not
he	me		people
	like		make
	then		could
	were	them	or
it	all	if	can
they	go	her	
would		one	
is		because	very
in		do	play
have	get	school	some
that	there	got	what

this

your

again

am

time

every

try

it's

home

didn't

way

wanted

going

two

found

good

dog

well

bed

as

help

love

money

mother

off

why

down

an

even

their

also

thing

never

house

around

work

girl

back

class

away

charge

started

where

each

came

now

boy

everyone

from

think

another

room

friends

come

sister

too

take

ran

any

other

nice

only

teacher

first

really

that's

best

food

after

put

sometimes

favorite

don't

how

football

brother

our

called

long

no

man

father

year

just

Mom

something

game

has

who

took

most

lot

tell

cat

fun

over

old

homework

things

Dad

once

games

by

family

new

thought

name

children

little

next

much

should

know

night

car

bad

want

into

Christmas

saw

many

made

water

friend

let

run

clean

did

eat

years

parents

more

give

before

see

told

team

better

big

world

kids

I'm

us

right

always

live

bus	swimming	knew	fish
say	keep	scared	goes
morning	buy	boys	trees
still		soon	coming
here	heard	read	dream
looked	than	lunch	gave
while	getting	store	outside
left	end		sleep
stop	I'd	whole	boat
air	last	balloons	grader
	named	call	
can't	talk	sea	tree
three	couldn't	horses	president
happy	books	baseball	TV
everybody		later	playing
everything	stay	men	must
until	girls	bear	show
asked	hard	real	afraid
different	which		gets
place	yes	start	dogs
sure	hit	almost	street
	person	pretty	
need	animals	high	cars
great	through	same	learn
door	fell	care	he's
life		few	tried
look	played	horse	candy
someone	wish	decided	fight
ball	watch	hurt	likes
days	being		snow
wouldn't	kind	book	done
story	walking	doing	use
	white	black	
find	important	ride	baby
finally	hope	walk	basketball
together	mean	gas	circus
lived		Mr.	four
anything	week	teachers	lost
every	might	wasn't	mad
been	lots	these	clothes

grade
ready
trip

turned
won
does
probably
died
fast
own
walked
ask
land

maybe
nothing
running
you're
may
both
city
ship
Friday
grow

red
broke
job
looking
small
today
having
jump
ok
planet

hour
all
myself

oh
earth
hill
summer
beautiful
funny
happened

park
upon
eighth
comes
war
feet
set

without
bring
country

ate
caught
five
change
responsibilities
they're
field

lady
Mrs.
turn

animal
enough
times
free
head
sports
build
except
bike
half

America
leave
move
police
states
feel
stuff
united
miss
suddenly

teach
catch
fire
party
doesn't
hair
pick
reason
second
winter

rest
kept
sit
eyes
top
trouble
fix
front
else
hot

math
seen
shot
dinner
its
sick
since

space
sport
schools

Thanksgiving
ground
such
sudden
trying
used
future
music
problem
seventh

weeks
won't
liked
lives
stopped
talking
throw
win
woke
yard

believe
God
let's
mouse
cut
killed
making
riding
rules
become

Appendix D

Words Most Commonly Misspelled
in Children's Writing

Word	Misspelling	Word	Misspelling
a lot	alot	basketball	basket ball
a while	awhile	because	becase
again	agian	because	becaus
again	agin	because	becouse
all right	alright	because	becuse
also	allso	because	cause
always	allways	before	befor
am	an	believe	belive
and	a	bigger	biger
and	an	black hole	blackhole
		buy	by
and	in		
another	a nother	came	cane
any more	anymore	can't	cant
anyone	any one	cannot	can not
anything	any thing	captain	captian
anyway	any way	charge	carge
around	arond	charge	charg
balloons	ballons	choir	chior

Word	Misspelling	Word	Misspelling
Christmas	Chrismas	friends	frinds
classroom	class room	get	git
clothes	cloths	getting	geting
		happened	happend
		happily	happly
clothes	close	have	hav
didn't	did'nt	he's	hes
didn't	didnt	heard	herd
different	diffrent	her	he
dogs	dog's	here	hear
don't	dont	hero	heroe
down	dan	heroes	heros
downstairs	down stair	him	hem
eighth	eigth	him	hin
etc.	ect	his	he's
		his	hes
		his	is
every	evey	homework	home work
every day	everyday	hurt	hert
everybody	every body	I'd	Id
everyone	every one		
everything	every thing	I'll	Ill
everywhere	every where	I'm	Im
fair	fare	in	i
family	famly	in charge	incharge
fell	fel	Indians	Indens
field	feild	inside	in side
		instead	insted
finally	finaly	into	in to
finally	finely	it's	its
first	frist	its	it's
football	foot ball		
found	fond	knew	new
friend	freind	know	no
friend's	friends	know	now
friends	freinds	let's	lets
friends	frends	little	littel
friends	friend's	lying	laying

Word	Misspelling	Word	Misspelling
make	mack	something	somthing
Mayflower	May flower	sometimes	some times
me	my	sometimes	somtimes
might	mite	started	stared
		stopped	stoped
millimeter	milimeter	stretch	strech
mother's	mothers	sure	share
myself	my self	swimming	swiming
new	now	teacher	techer
no	know	than	then
now	know		
off	of		
once	ones	that's	thats
one	on	their	ther
or	ore	their	there
		their	thier
our	are	them	then
outside	out side	then	than
passed	past	then	the
people	peaple	there	their
people	peopl	there	ther
people's	peoples	they	tay
Pilgrims	Pilgrams		
play	paly		
popped	poped	they	thae
probably	probly	they	thay
really	realy	they	the
		they're	their
		they're	there
said	sed	to	too
said	siad	today	to day
said	side	too	to
Saturday	Saterday	turkey	turky
school	shcool	two	to
school	shool		
she's	shes		
some	som	two	tow
some	sum	until	untill
someone	some one	upon	apon

131

Word	Misspelling	Word	Misspelling
we're	were	whole	hole
went	want	with	whith
went	wet	with	wiht
went	whent	won't	wont
were	where	world	wold
what's	whats		
whatever	what ever	would	wode
		would	wold
when	wen	would	wood
when	win	would	woud
whenever	when ever	would	wud
where	were	wouldn't	wouldnt
while	wile	you're	your

Books about Process Writing and Spelling

ATWELL, NANCIE. *In the Middle: Writing, Reading and Learning with Adolescents*. Portsmouth, NH: Boynton-Cook, 1987.

BISSEX, GLENDA. *GNYS AT WRK: A Child Learns to Write and Read*. Cambridge, MA: Harvard University Press, 1980.

CALKINS, LUCY MCCORMICK. *Lessons from a Child: On the Teaching and Learning of Writing*. Portsmouth, NH: Heinemann, 1983.

————. *The Art of Teaching Writing*. Portsmouth, NH: Heinemann, 1986.

————. *Living Between the Lines*. Portsmouth, NH: Heinemann, 1991.

ELBOW, PETER. *Writing with Power*. New York: Oxford University Press, 1981.

GENTRY, J. RICHARD. *Spel . . . Is A Four-Letter Word*. Portsmouth, NH: Heinemann, 1987.

GRAVES, DONALD H. *Discover Your Own Literacy*. Portsmouth, NH: Heinemann, 1990.

————. *Writing: Teachers and Children at Work*. Portsmouth, NH: Heinemann, 1983.

NATHAN, RUTH, FRANCES TEMPLE, KATHLEEN JUNTUNEN, and CHARLES TEMPLE. *Classroom Strategies That Work: An Elementary Teacher's Guide to Process Writing*. Portsmouth, NH: Heinemann, 1989.

TEMPLE, CHARLES, RUTH NATHAN, NANCY BURRIS, and FRANCES TEMPLE. *The Beginnings of Writing*. 2nd ed. Needham Heights, MA: Allyn & Bacon, 1988.

WILDE, SANDRA. *You Kan Red This!* Portsmouth, NH: Heinemann, 1992.

References

ATWELL, NANCIE. 1987. *In the Middle: Writing, Reading and Learning with Adolescents*. Portsmouth, NH: Boynton-Cook.

BISSEX, GLENDA L. 1980. *GNYS AT WRK: A Child Learns to Write and Read*. Cambridge, MA: Harvard University Press.

CHOMSKY, NOAM, and MORRIS HALLE. 1968. *The Sound Pattern of English*. New York: Harper and Row.

CUMMINGS, DONALD WAYNE. 1988. *American English Spelling*. Baltimore: The Johns Hopkins University Press.

CUNNINGHAM, PAT. *Phonics They Use*. New York: HarperCollins, 1991.

FISHER, J. H. 1977. "Chancery and the Emergence of Standard Written English in the Fifteenth Century." *Speculum*. 870–99.

GENTRY, J. RICHARD. 1978. "Early Spelling Strategies." *The Elementary School Journal* 79:88–92.

———. 1982. "An Analysis of Developmental Spelling in GNYS AT WRK." *The Reading Teacher* 36(2):192–200.

———. 1985. "You Can Analyze Developmental Spelling." *Teaching K-8*. 15(9):44–45.

GIBSON, ELEANOR, and HARRY LEVIN. 1975. *The Psychology of Reading*. Cambridge, MA: The MIT Press.

HENDERSON, EDMUND H., and JAMES W. BEERS. 1980. *Developmental and Cognitive Aspects of Learning to Spell*. Newark, DE: International Reading Association.

• REFERENCES •

HOLDAWAY, DON. 1979. *The Foundations of Literacy*. New York: Ashton Scholastic.

JONGSMA, KATHLEEN, ed. 1990. "Questions and Answers: Reading-Spelling Links." *The Reading Teacher* 43(8):608–9.

READ, CHARLES. 1975. *Children's Categorizations of Speech Sounds in English*. Urbana, IL: National Council of Teachers of English.

READ, CHARLES, and RICHARD E. HODGES. 1983. Spelling. In *Encyclopedia of Educational Research*. 5th ed. New York: Macmillan.

SAMUELS, M. 1963. "Some Applications of Middle English Dialectology." *English Studies* 44:81–94.

SMITH, CARL B. and GARY M. INGERSOLL. 1984. *Written Vocabulary of Elementary School Pupils, Ages* 6–14. Indiana University School of Education. *Monographs on Language and Reading Studies* No. 6, January.

SMITH, P. 1976. *Jefferson: A Revealing Biography*. New York: American Heritage Publishing Co.

TEMPLETON, SHANE. 1979. "Spelling First, Sound Later: The Relationship Between Spelling and Higher Order Phonological Knowledge in Older Students." *Research in the Teaching of English* 13:69–80.

VENEZKY, RICHARD. 1970. *The Structure of English Orthography*. The Hague, Netherlands: Mouthon.